9 | 19 | 23

BATTLE
for the
COLUMBIA RIVER

BATTLE
for the
COLUMBIA RIVER

THE RISE OF THE
OREGON STEAM NAVIGATION COMPANY

Cheers!

Mychal Ostler

MYCHAL OSTLER, MA, LMFT

FOREWORD BY TOM CRAMBLETT,
CAPTAIN OF THE STERNWHEELER *COLUMBIA GORGE*

THE
History
PRESS

Published by The History Press
Charleston, SC
www.historypress.com

Front cover, top: courtesy of Shutterstock; *bottom*: courtesy of Oregon Historical Society.
Back cover: courtesy of Oregon Historical Society; *insert*: author's collection.

First published 2023

Manufactured in the United States

ISBN 9781467154086

Library of Congress Control Number: 2022951603

Notice: The information in this book is true and complete to the best of our knowledge. It is offered without guarantee on the part of the author or The History Press. The author and The History Press disclaim all liability in connection with the use of this book.

To my wife, Nora, whose encouragement, belief in my potential as a writer and enthusiasm for my unconventional ideas inspired me to achieve the goals of which I am most proud. This book exists because of you.

CONTENTS

CONTENTS

FOREWORD

Ever since my family moved to the Cascades in the 1880s, our lives have been intertwined with the Columbia River. More than half of my own life's journey, almost forty years, has been spent on the river as the captain of a replica Columbia Gorge stern-wheeler. The determination of John C. Ainsworth and his partners to succeed in building a transportation empire based in the Northwest as the eastern United States was embroiled in the Civil War is admirable. While I may not agree with Ainsworth's methods in building his empire, my love for the Cascades, for piloting a stern-wheeler up and down the river and for the many moods of that magnificent river mirror his love.

Mychal Ostler was a crew member of the Columbia Gorge stern-wheeler that I captained. His work on the boat and the stories I could relate to him spurred his research into the history of the Oregon Steam Navigation Company. While I knew the major events of the history of the OSN, I learned so much about the beginning and growth through this definitive book. From

Lewis and Clark's exploration in 1805 until Ainsworth's resignation from the OSN board in 1879, the expansion of the Pacific Northwest transportation, mining and agricultural industries flowed through the Cascades. It is the heart of the Gorge.

—Tom Cramblett
November 2022

PREFACE

How does one become so enamored with a nineteenth-century transportation company that they choose to write a book about it?

They grow up immersed in that company's history.

I spent my youth in Skamania County, Washington, in the heart of the Columbia River Gorge. In this remote area, the Columbia, like the space it occupies in the landscape, maintains a prominent presence in the minds of local citizens. Watersport athletes, fishing enthusiasts and outdoor recreationalists study the river's surface and make their daily plans around the Columbia's movements.

Like everyone else I knew, I cultivated a relationship with the river. Starting at an early age, I spent afternoons at the water's edge, absorbing all the sensory stimuli that nature had to offer and filling the vast, empty physical space above and beneath the surface of the river with my imagination. For me, the Columbia became a reliable, safe and comforting metaphorical space to connect with both the natural world and my inner world.

As I aged and began to notice the more human aspects of the river, I became interested in the many watercraft that traversed its surface. Watching these vessels appear and disappear from sight became a thrilling sport for a young boy. I studied the grain barges as they honked their way past the fishing boats in their path, the cruise ships with their sleek lines and the occasional flashy yacht.

But it was the watercraft that I saw in the photos on display at the local history museums and visitor centers that became my obsession. I spent countless hours staring at these photos and recreating them with hand illustrations at home. I was enthralled with the physical presence of the steamboats, their size and their construction designs. To me, these photos seemed a portal into another world; unrecognizable, because the time period was so long ago, yet intimately familiar, because in the background of every photo could be seen the same geographical landmarks that were a part of my daily life. Of all the steamboats I viewed in the photos, it was those built and owned by the Oregon Steam Navigation Company (OSN) that struck me as the most majestic. Like the interpreters before me, these appeared to me more like "floating palaces" than boats.

When I grew old enough to work, I sought employment where I could be as close to the river as possible and nurture my relationship with it. I was offered a job as deckhand on the stern-wheeler *Columbia Gorge*, a tour boat and replica of the steamboats I studied in my favorite historical photos. It was during my shifts on the stern-wheeler that I met Captain Tom Cramblett, who not only looked the part of the captains I saw in the photos, but was also himself at the wheel of the vessel. Captain Tom cultivated in me the technical skills needed to perform my job and, between tasks, also cultivated my interest in the OSN. Like a teacher, Captain Tom shared his knowledge with me about the company, recommended literature as homework assignments and joined me on a trip to Reed College, where we reviewed the OSN's surviving business records together and discussed our discoveries and inferences.

I SOUGHT EMPLOYMENT OFF the boat in 2010 and moved out of Skamania County. After relocating to North Carolina six years later, I was farther away than I had ever been from my oldest and dearest childhood friend, the Columbia River.

But despite the thousands of miles between me and the waters where its steamboats plied, I grew closer to the OSN than ever before. It was in my new home on the East Coast that I plunged deeper into the history of OSN, beneath the appearances of the steamboats in my favorite photos and inside the bowels of the company itself—its employees, management policies, financial practices and the relationships between these and the social and physical environment that surrounded the company during its existence.

To understand and appreciate these intangible aspects of the OSN, I applied the same energy and enthusiasm I utilized when studying and replicating images of the company's steamboats as a child. I engaged in what I imagined a cold-case file detective might do: pursuing leads, reviewing documents for clues, critically reviewing contemporary interpretations and researching the backgrounds and activities of the individuals connected with the company. Individual questions led to several more, and the more I learned, the more I wanted to know about not only the OSN's steamboats but also the people connected with the company.

As my research of the OSN progressed, a story gradually revealed itself. The plot and characters materialized, and I stumbled upon all the elements of a timeless tale: villains and heroes who contended with greed, fear, tragedy, sacrifice, triumph, irony, scandal and deep fraternal bonds, all occurring within the OSN Board of Directors. The company's executive leadership team—the main characters of the story—seemed to be speaking to me through the documents they left behind. In their writing, I discovered each individual's fears, ambitions, traumas, behavior patterns, worldviews, ideas, preferences and impressions of others. The more I learned about these people, the more I empathized with their views.

I felt increasingly compelled to share the story I uncovered in my research. In performing my literature review, I was shocked to learn that, although many articles, academic studies and chapters in books had been written about the history of the OSN, in the nearly 150 years since the company's existence, not a single book had been published about the subject. Captain Tom, one of the few Columbia Gorge locals with whom I had remained in contact after leaving the Pacific Northwest, was equally perplexed. We agreed during a phone conversation one evening that someone should write such a book, so that the story of the OSN could be made more accessible to the general public. Given my history and interest in the topic, I could find no reason why I should not make the effort.

WRITING THIS BOOK HAS been one of the most meaningful projects of my life.

Far more than securing a publishing contract, my reward was participating in the processes of researching and telling the OSN's story from beginning to end. These processes, which required a significant amount of time and mental energy, were challenging, but also exciting, humbling, cathartic, even addictive. Writing this book allowed me the opportunity to reconnect with and celebrate some of the most important aspects of my childhood and share these aspects with others. In some ways, I experience a sense of loss when I reflect on the fact that the work is complete.

My greatest hope is that research of the OSN is never complete. I do not wish for this book to serve as a definitive history of the company or even that I be considered an expert on the subject. Instead, I wish that my writing may serve simply as a presentation of ideas and contributions to an ongoing, open dialogue about the OSN, one that I hope will continue in a public forum long after the publication of this book. If historians challenge my interpretations of the story and its characters with sources, facts and contextual variables that I overlooked in my research, so much the better. Their arguments will be important additions to the conversation and provide a richer understanding and appreciation of the OSN.

ACKNOWLEDGEMENTS

Like every meaningful journey on which I have embarked throughout my life, the writing of this book has involved the assistance and guidance of many individuals. Because their contributions are irreplaceable to and shaped the vision and execution of this project, I consider it my duty to directly and thoroughly credit them here so that the reader may bear them in mind when reading the story.

First and foremost, I must thank Captain Tom Cramblett, who shares my lifelong passion for the history of the OSN and who supplied me with much encouragement and motivation throughout the entire project.

To Robert Freeze, I am indebted for insisting that I persist and be creative in my efforts to publish when I became discouraged with previous rejections.

In my childhood friend, Dr. Kelly Johnson, I found a relatable model for launching a successful career in professional writing and becoming a published author.

Invaluable to my research was Nanosh Lucas, whose timely, reliable and expert assistance with accessing and interpreting the John C. Ainsworth Papers at the University of Oregon helped form much of the story outlined in the following pages.

Also invaluable to my research was the assistance of Siany Hennessey, whose communicative, thorough and energetic service at the Oregon Historical Society archives provided irreplaceable primary source context about specific members of the OSN Board of Directors.

Finally, this book would not exist without the efforts of Laurie Krill, whose visionary talents and belief in the story's potential guided my manuscript throughout the entire publication process.

INTRODUCTION

I t was a June day in Portland, Oregon, in 1879, and John Ainsworth, president of the Oregon Steam Navigation Company (OSN), was at work in his third-story office at the company's downtown headquarters. At his office door appeared a tall, burly, mustached German named Henry Villard.

Together, Ainsworth and Villard presented a stark contrast. Outwardly, Ainsworth was Villard's inferior. At age fifty-seven, Ainsworth was considered elderly and looked diminutive with his graying hair, slight frame and short stature. Ainsworth's manners were equally unintimidating. Where Villard enjoyed a national reputation as a gifted writer and commanding orator, Ainsworth, typically quiet during social gatherings, exhibited a diffident affect punctuated with subtle, congenial expressions. He both wrote and spoke using simple, unassuming language.

In addition to his physical presence, Villard was confident that his celebrity status and newfound wealth would dominate Ainsworth during their meeting. Already famous on the East Coast for his journalism career, Villard had spent the previous decade adding fortune to his fame by making money for and off of investors on Wall Street and in Europe, brokering their trades in the lively American railroad securities market. Over the previous five years, Villard's success and net worth had accelerated at an impressive rate as he traded larger and larger blocks of equities. By the late 1870s, Villard and his syndicates owned controlling interests in several West Coast transportation companies. Next, he turned his attention to the OSN, judging it a natural addition to his portfolio.

Despite the fame, power and money Villard had earned on both sides of the Atlantic, not many on the Pacific coast had ever heard of him. Ainsworth had but was not impressed with Villard or his aristocratic associates. Villard made a trip to Portland a few years earlier and made an offer to buy the OSN, but Ainsworth rejected it without bothering to submit a counteroffer. Now Villard was back at the OSN offices to try again.

After Villard greeted Ainsworth at the door, he was floored when Ainsworth hijacked the conversation: "I don't know whether to invite you to take a seat in this office or not." Ainsworth proceeded to scold Villard for his attorney's behavior. Ainsworth had heard that the man bragged around Portland that Villard planned on starting a transportation company to compete directly with the OSN and that the enterprise was to be bankrolled by none other than Jay Gould, New York's most notorious financial market manipulator. Ainsworth made clear that he would not be intimidated. "We are not in a position to be crushed out," he gruffly informed Villard. "We were here first."

Having drawn his battle lines, Ainsworth finally invited Villard to sit. He asked Villard to present his offer to purchase the OSN. Villard rationalized that he judged all assets to possess a value of $1 million. Ainsworth immediately rejected this, and when Villard probed Ainsworth for details about the OSN's recent operations, Ainsworth rejected Villard again, citing company policy as preventing him from disclosing such details. Villard protested that he could not form a credible opinion of the company's value if he did not know more about its operation.

Well aware that Villard understood much less about railroads and steamboats than he did their stocks and bonds, Ainsworth was convinced that if Villard's engineers could examine for themselves the quality of the OSN's operation, Villard would realize the company's true value. To that end, Ainsworth proposed a condition to continue negotiations: if Villard and his engineers would travel the line of the OSN and perform a thorough appraisal of its assets, Ainsworth would name a price to sell the business. Left with no other choice, Villard agreed.

VILLARD AND HIS ENTOURAGE began their journey on the OSN line in high style, boarding the pride of the company's fleet, the steamboat *Wide West*. This floating palace received the group from the OSN's two-story

4-4-0 locomotive *J. S. Ruckel* and its twin, *S.G. Reed*, operated on the OSN's portage railroad at the Cascades. *Courtesy of Oregon Historical Society*.

wharf at Portland and steamed down the Willamette River and up the Columbia at a cruising speed of just under twenty miles per hour. As the giant stern-wheeler churned through the gateway to the Columbia Gorge, the romantic Villard would have no doubt been reminded of the Bavarian Alps of his native country when he and his party gazed up at the tall basalt towers flanking waterfalls to starboard and the majesty of Beacon Rock, Hamilton and Table Mountains to port. When Villard visited Oregon five years before, he had become infatuated with the Willamette Valley and the views of Mount Hood and Mount Saint Helens from downtown Portland. The trip up the gorge only increased his affection for the Pacific Northwest.

After the stern-wheeler's towering bow nosed against the OSN's floating wharf at lower Cascades, Washington Territory, Villard and his entourage disembarked and boarded a long passenger car hitched to a hissing 4-4-0 locomotive, which stood by at the company railroad depot at the crest of the riverbank. The train bore the men along the shoreline of an increasingly narrowing and turbulent Columbia, across tall trestles and between deep cuts to the eastern terminus of the railroad, six miles upstream. The men craned their necks to discover the source of a heavy roar, which increased in volume during the final mile of the ride, a cataract known as the Upper Cascades rapids. On the other side of the tracks was more OSN railroad property: car houses, shops and a turntable, all well maintained and in good working order. Here, another large stern-wheeler picked up the Villard party at the railroad's terminus for their cruise to The Dalles, Oregon.

After the passengers finished their tour of the gorge, the steamer chugged toward a quaint hamlet extending from the banks of a large bend in the river. As the city of The Dalles came into view, it was immediately noticeable that the OSN dominated the cityscape. A large floating wharf and warehouse rose from the water. Beyond these were the company machine shops, railroad yard, offices and rolling stock. Though these were buildings constructed for industrial use, they wore fresh coats of paint and were designed with trendy Victorian elements such as moldings, peak ornaments, transoms and hooded doors. The group transferred again from steamboat to plush passenger car, pulled by another modern locomotive over a fourteen-mile railroad that penetrated an increasingly arid landscape.

At the railroad's terminus at Celilo, Oregon, another community dominated by the OSN and adjacent to an even more violent cataract than at Cascades, yet another well-appointed stern-wheeler awaited Villard and his men. Before climbing the gangplank for the final leg of their journey, the

The Dalles–Celilo portage railroad, constructed by the OSN to bypass an unnavigable stretch of the Columbia River east of The Dalles. *Courtesy of Oregon Historical Society.*

party could have placed a call to The Dalles office on the OSN's telephone, a novel device rarely seen at that time on the West Coast and one of three lines connecting services on the company's Columbia route.

On the cruise to Walla Walla, Villard and his engineers took in new vistas, where high cliffs gave way to the rolling hills of the Palouse. Here teemed healthy wheat, the current crop predicted to produce a record harvest during the coming autumn. When reaped and sacked, the wheat would make its way to the riverbank, where OSN warehouses, wharves, steamboats and railcars would groan under its weight. Villard learned that this commodity had not only become Portland's most valuable international export but had also become the most valuable generator of profit for the OSN.

AFTER HIS TOUR UP the Columbia River, Villard returned to OSN headquarters. Now satisfied that Villard was a serious buyer, Ainsworth opened up the company's books.

As Villard pored over nineteen years of accounting ledgers and journals, the numbers on the pages told the story of how the OSN came to dominate the Columbia for nearly two consecutive decades. During his review, it quickly became clear to Villard why Ainsworth rejected his initial valuation of the company. There was the real estate portfolio, which included the most desirable lots in major cities lining the Willamette and Columbia Rivers, commercial structures and undeveloped acreage, valued at over $2 million. The company's floating stock, which included a total of twenty-six steamboats, ten barges, other vessels and several wharves, was valued at just under $750,000. The rest of the company's hard assets, including its rolling stock, four railroads, equipment, a canal and a navigation lock at Oregon City, was worth just over $700,000. Paper assets consisted of four thousand shares of OSN stock containing a par value of $2 million. Throughout its existence, the OSN appeared to have never issued a single bond, and Villard could find no trace of other debt, save for loans totaling no more than $300,000, taken out at the time of the company's incorporation and paid back promptly. After this, the OSN remained debt-free for the next seventeen years.

Perhaps more compelling to Villard than the OSN's collection of boats, trains, buildings and land was the company's ability to make money. Villard found that in the OSN's third year alone, earnings were $1.3 million, an unprecedented amount at the time for a business on the remote Pacific Northwest frontier. The OSN also demonstrated an ability to produce not only substantial but also consistent profits, generating such large quantities of surplus capital at any given time that the company easily purchased competitors with cash, provided their own funds for expansion and had paid its shareholders a total of nearly $5 million in dividends. Based on trending monthly profits, Villard calculated that the OSN was on track to net $1 million for the current year, a figure sure to impress his investors in the East and across the Atlantic.

WHEN VILLARD FINISHED HIS examination of the OSN's financials, Ainsworth re-initiated negotiations for the sale.

Enlightened with an insider's view of the company's value and how expensive it would be, even for the likes of Jay Gould, to compete with it, Villard knew Ainsworth possessed all the leverage. Ainsworth listed his terms, and in less than thirty minutes, the two men reached an agreement. Villard gave Ainsworth everything he wanted: conditions, contract language and, most important, price and form of payment: $5 million, half of which would be paid as stocks and bonds of Villard's new company and the remaining half as cash. Villard even agreed to pay a $100,000 deposit, nonrefundable if Villard failed to deliver $1.9 million in cash within thirty days. After signing their agreement, Villard returned to New York, and to Ainsworth's surprise and slight chagrin—he was counting on pocketing the $100,000—Villard made the payment on time.

Word about the sale of the OSN spread quickly on the streets of Portland, and local newspaper reporters chased the story. After discrediting the hearsay that the homegrown enterprise was the latest victim of Jay Gould, the press applauded Ainsworth's deal as a blessing for regional trade, citing trust in Villard and his plans for the property. The *Morning Oregonian* captured the mood of some Portlanders about the sale in an article that read more like a eulogy than a report of a business transaction. Of the company's assets, the author declared that they were "the greatest in the northwest." Of Ainsworth and his management team, the author was more succinct: "The pre-eminence of our city...is largely due to their investment, interest and management."

TWO YEARS LATER, AINSWORTH, with his characteristic modesty when describing his most significant achievements, counted the sale of the OSN merely as a "financial success." His words did not capture the true gravity of the event. For Ainsworth, who started life as a poor orphan who spent his nights sleeping under the desk of a country store and launched his career on the West Coast with just nine dollars in his pocket, the multimillion-dollar deal was the crowning achievement of his life.

Ainsworth's company was formed of similarly precarious and humble circumstances. The OSN was created with a capital of just $172,000— what Ainsworth described later as the "highest possible figure" representing the value of a small collection of ramshackle steamboats—and a group of managers who could barely get through a meeting without shouting threats at one another, much less work as a team. From its inception, Ainsworth, as he had done during his previous career as a steamboat captain, skillfully guided the OSN around the obstacles typical of businesses in their early stages. The OSN not only survived, it also grew exponentially more powerful and rich throughout two tumultuous decades that included a civil war, several economic contractions, a failed buyout, fierce competition, an internal coup, hostile political attacks and environmental disasters.

With its long history, powerful resources and extensive operations, the OSN became integral to the economic, geographic and social development of the Pacific Northwest. It was the OSN that introduced modern railroads, advanced marine engineering and both the telegraph and telephone to the region. These revolutionary conveniences and the OSN's multimodal transportation system helped spur settlement of the Northwest interior. As Oregon's and Washington's largest employer, the OSN paid wages that funded many households along the Columbia River from Astoria to Lewiston, and the compensation for executives and shareholders made its way back into local microeconomies in the form of consumption of merchandise and services, capital for smaller businesses, real estate development and even the launching and maintenance of philanthropic endeavors. Taxes assessed on the OSN's valuable property and revenue generated by the company provided critical sources of funding for the state, county and city governments that lined the Columbia and Willamette Rivers.

But the OSN did not win unanimous approval from the public. Farmers complained persistently and increasingly loudly about exorbitant freight rates, competitors were nearly ruined by Ainsworth's ruthless defense of the OSN's territory and claimants were exasperated by evasion. To Democrats and those against the corporate expansion policy championed by the Lincoln administration, the OSN's rise to power, the untouchable monopoly it created and the wealth of its stockholders represented the destruction of a Jacksonian utopia they came west to create.

For Republicans and Portland business owners, the OSN represented local patriotism, a tangible measurement of modern progress and a critical means to ending the Northwest's decades-long struggle for economic independence from California. For those who made fortunes off their involvement with the OSN, the company's success represented what came to be recognized as the American dream, where an organization and its managers could begin from the most meager of circumstances and achieve wealth and status in a single generation.

I

THE RIVER AT WAR

The year 1859 was a tense one for the eastern United States. Attention was fixated on the interminable slavery controversy, and all eyes were on the South. What was once a lively debate was now a national crisis; Bleeding Kansas entered its fifth year, and radical abolitionists raided the federal arsenal at Harpers Ferry, resulting in several deaths and the execution of antislavery idol John Brown.

Lighter news from the western territories created a timely diversion for an anxious American public. There were the annual gold strikes, at Pikes Peak in Colorado and at the Comstock Lode in Utah. In the Pacific Northwest, a border dispute between the United States and Britain, dubbed the "Pig War," began and ended with a single nonhuman casualty. On the Puget Sound, the city of Olympia was incorporated, and farther south, Oregon was admitted to the Union as its thirty-third state.

In addition to the gold strikes, steady immigration and a robust military presence significantly increased Oregon's population throughout the 1840s and '50s. Of its major population centers in the late 1850s, which included Astoria, Portland, Oregon City and The Dalles, Portland was the newest and experiencing the fastest growth. Located about twelve miles up the Willamette River from its confluence with the Columbia, Portland sprang up along the western shoreline and out of a thick stand of Douglas fir trees packed to the water's edge.

In 1859, Portland was in the middle of a major transition. After more than a decade of political dysfunction, its nearly three thousand

Portland, Oregon waterfront in 1858. *Courtesy of Oregon Historical Society.*

inhabitants were finally beginning to enjoy the benefits of a cooperative government, such as the creation of a police force and the construction of a jail. Preceding this development, Portland's various public service positions had been exploited by the city's merchants, who, since the late 1840s, had secured political power mostly for the purpose of advancing their private business interests.

The strategy worked well for the merchants, who enriched themselves and drove the economic development of Portland throughout the 1850s. In 1857 alone, they exported over $3 million in flour, pork and lumber. In 1858, the merchants capitalized on a windfall when the Fraser River gold rush funneled throngs of prospectors and opportunists through Portland's muddy thoroughfares and into the rough-hewn doors of the shops lining Front Street, Portland's first business district. The economic momentum of the late '50s produced so much disposable income for Portland's most successful merchants that they erected the most expensive and stylish commercial and residential structures yet seen in the city. Society improved, too, at least by prevailing Victorian standards, as attendance at wedding receptions, luncheons, fraternal meetings, dinner parties, dances and church functions increased.

The Steamboat Business

The Fraser River gold rush also benefited steamboat owners, who collected huge profits from their vessels' transport of men, animals, equipment and foodstuffs to the British Columbia mining districts. Immediately after the news spread about the discovery of gold in the north, a stampede ensued for the safest, fastest and most reliable means of travel to the mines, which in 1858 was the fleet of small steamboats plying the Columbia and Willamette Rivers. Almost overnight, customer demand outpaced the number of steamboats available. Owners made as much money as their boats could make trips, charging as much as the frantic market would bear for passenger tickets and freight fees.

But the Fraser River rush was short-lived. At the beginning of 1859, the prospectors had moved on to newer strikes elsewhere in the West, creating a vacuum in demand for Northwest products and services that threw the regional economy into a slump. What had before been a torrent of river traffic was now a mere trickle: there were suddenly too many boats competing for too few customers.

As steamboat owners readjusted to these market conditions, old operating problems resurfaced. There was the cost of fuel, which, because of the extensive labor required to fell trees and process them into cords for boilers, had remained so high that it was often a challenge for owners to break even on their expenses for a single trip. Other recurring overhead costs, such as salaries for skilled labor, machinery repairs and the shipping of replacement parts from the East, placed even more financial strain on steamboat owners.

The cost of fuel was excessive under normal conditions and nearly financially ruinous when unexpected events demanded higher rates of consumption. The amount of wood—the principal fuel source available for steam power across the Northwest until the twentieth century—required to power Columbia steamboats was significant, especially on stretches of the river where the channel narrowed and the current strengthened. Consumption multiplied when a steamboat grounded on a reef or sandbar, a regular occurrence due to the constantly shifting riverbed, lack of navigational charts, fluctuating water levels and compromised visibility during the fire and fog seasons. The pioneers and Native Americans who lived near the river became privy to the market for steamboat fuel and exploited it accordingly, raising prices and lying about quantities as opportunities presented themselves.

But Columbia River steamboat owners faced many more problems in 1859 than high overhead costs and a lack of customers. The most urgent challenges were presented by poor management decisions, inexperienced crews, hostile relations between competing owners and, most significant, the fact that the success or failure of every steamboat operation between Astoria and The Dalles was determined by a six-mile stretch of river called the Cascades.

TRANSPORTATION AT THE CASCADES

Forty miles east of the Willamette River mouth and in between where the town of North Bonneville and Ashes Lake are located today is a section of the Columbia that was known throughout the nineteenth century as the Cascades. Though the river's current is now carefully regulated by Bonneville Dam, until its completion in 1938, this six-mile stretch of narrow, shallow and meandering channel was highly dangerous. Meriwether Lewis and William Clark gave the Cascades its English name during their legendary voyage downstream in the fall of 1805. On landing their party near present-day Ashes Lake, Lewis and Clark surveyed a giant rapid, where the river abruptly constricted into a boulder, island and reef-strewn chute, dividing the violent water in all directions as it traversed the obstructions. This rapid and the shores surrounding it came to be known as the "Upper Cascades." One mile downriver, near the current location of Fort Rains, the explorers found another rapid, this one tamer, that they named the "Middle Cascades." A mile farther downstream, where the Bonneville Dam spillway stands today, was located a third rapid, this one the least turbulent of the three. This longer, wider and safer reach came to be known as the "Lower Cascades."

Lewis and Clark found the Upper and Middle Cascades rapids unnavigable; riding the current downriver could be fatal, and attempting to overcome it by heading upriver was a futile effort. Under the guidance of local Native Americans, the explorers portaged around the Upper and Middle rapids by following a trail that ran along a bluff skirting the north bank of the river, near the present path of Highway 14.

Navigating the Upper and Middle Cascades rapids was no easier forty years after the Lewis and Clark expedition. Oregon Trail immigrants occasionally attempted to float their crude rafts through the white water; these were quickly dashed to pieces, drowning their passengers. To avoid

Above: Upper Cascades rapids, looking north. This mile-long stretch of white water could not be ascended by any watercraft until Bonneville Dam was completed. *Courtesy of Oregon Historical Society.*

Left: Navigation obstructions at Middle Cascades. Before the 1890s, steamboats rarely passed this dangerous point on the Columbia River. *Courtesy of Oregon Historical Society.*

such catastrophes, the Upper Cascades became a natural rendezvous point for immigrant parties as they paused to file onto the north shore trail, rest their animals, tend to their sick or bury their dead. Some chose to end their long journey west and homestead along the shoreline just above the rapids or downriver on a sprawling meadow at the Lower Cascades.

The necessity of portaging around the rapids presented business opportunities for the energetic and industrious Cascades settler. Mired throughout the winter and spring in slippery mud and clouded with dust during the summer, there was ample room for improvement of the forest trail along the shoreline. In 1850, Skamania County Donation Land claimant Francis Chenoweth took it upon himself during his first year of residence at the Cascades to improve the trail by constructing a plank road over it, to which he bolted wooden rails to support light carts. In an attempt to inaugurate a service to portage the entire six miles of rapids, Chenoweth experimented with sail power as a means of navigating the lower Cascades. Though it proved difficult to maintain control when traveling downstream, and making headway upstream was tedious, Chenoweth found that a simple flat-bottomed barge rigged with a sail could overcome the Lower Cascades rapid under the right weather conditions. After Chenoweth secured a few mules to pull the carts on his tramway and hired a local settler to run his sailboats, the first portage service at the Cascades was open for business.

Unfortunately for Chenoweth, he operated his portage service at such a loss that he eventually sold his business to salvage a portion of his investment. Having missed the peak of the immigration season because his tramway was under construction, his portage service was not ready to receive customers until autumn, when traffic volume had begun to slack. To survive at the Cascades, Chenoweth was forced to abandon the transportation industry and resume his previous career as a lawyer.

BRADFORD AND COMPANY

Luckily for Chenoweth, he found eager buyers in the Bradford brothers.

Daniel Flint and Putnam Flint Bradford settled at the Cascades early in 1850, after a six-month ocean voyage from New York. The brothers were born and raised in Sheffield, Massachusetts, by one of the most distinguished families on the East Coast. They were descendants of William Bradford, a passenger on the *Mayflower* who was elected by his fellow colonists as the first governor of Plymouth. Daniel and Putnam's father, James Bradford, was a famous and wealthy reverend in Sheffield, which allowed his family to enjoy an elevated status in southwestern Massachusetts society.

The brothers' motivations for immigrating west were similar to those of many other pioneers of the gold rush era. Like their peers, the brothers sought to deploy speculative schemes, make quick profits and return East with enough cash to enjoy financial independence, impress others with their material wealth and live the idyllic Victorian lifestyle of genteel leisure. Ahead of many pioneers in social standing and formal education, Daniel

OSN employees at The Dalles administrative office. Daniel Bradford is believed to be seated. *Courtesy of Oregon Historical Society.*

and Putnam arrived in the Pacific Northwest with high expectations and behaved as though they had much to prove.

Daniel bore the brunt of these expectations. Thirty-one years of age when he arrived at the Cascades, Daniel was older, more established and more experienced than his twenty-four-year-old brother. Daniel, who left a wife, son and career as a merchant back home in Sheffield, had much at stake in coming west. Putnam had little to lose in taking a chance at a new life on the frontier, but for Daniel, it was perhaps the most significant risk he had taken thus far, with his distant family to provide for and his vulnerable brother to protect.

After landing at the Cascades, the Bradford brothers immediately went to work proving themselves. They filed Donation Land Claims for prime riverfront property on the north shore, and within a couple of months, the brothers had established a general store and salmon fishing operation on their properties, purchased Chenoweth's tramway and doubled its length.

The Bradfords' boldest plan was to make history as builders of the first steamboat to ply between the Cascades and The Dalles. To fund the project, Daniel leveraged his confidence and persuasion skills to pitch the profit potential of his steamboat idea to a cousin in San Francisco, who, along with his merchant partners, agreed to extend the Bradfords capital for the venture. Daniel then promptly ordered a kit for a small steamboat from an East Coast manufacturer.

After the kit was delivered at the Lower Cascades, it was assembled on-site. Without sufficient power to overcome the rapids, the steamboat had to be transported to the calm waters above the Upper Cascades by land. To execute the seemingly impossible feat, lubricated wooden skids were wedged under the bow of the vessel, and heavy chains were attached to both the hull and a team of oxen on the shore. The animals dragged the steamboat over the skids until they could be pried loose and wedged under the bow again. The crew repeated this painful, hazardous and tedious process countless times over the six miles of rocky shoreline to the Upper Cascades.

After the ordeal, the sidewheel-propelled steamboat was christened *James P. Flint*, in honor of Daniel's cousin and investor, and was successfully launched. The *Flint* immediately began making trips shuttling passengers and freight between the Cascades and The Dalles. Daniel and Putnam's business, which they incorporated under the name Bradford and Company, secured its place in history as builder and operator of the first steamboat to navigate the Columbia River above the Cascades. It appeared as though the brothers had been successful in proving themselves in the West.

But like Chenoweth, it took only a few months for the Bradford brothers to learn just how hard it was to make a living at the Cascades. Though the *Flint* was launched in time to make the majority of the year's revenue during the busy season, it was not enough to meet Daniel's financial obligations. He and his partners eventually decided to sell to minimize losses. Daniel found a buyer in Portland, but when the *Flint* was on its way downstream to be delivered, she struck a reef and sank.

In the meantime, a series of catastrophic events descended on the Cascades community that put the Bradford brothers' business—and lives—at serious risk. A smallpox outbreak converted their settlement into a field hospital and mass graveyard, as the community surrendered every available structure to accommodate the sick and dying immigrants making their way downriver. After winter set in, a blizzard blew down the Columbia Gorge, dumping feet of snow and thick sheets of ice, which forced a shutdown of all Bradford and Company operations. Within days, most of the livestock sustaining settlers east of Fort Vancouver had died from hypothermia or starvation.

Though they suffered damage to their property and lost most of their livestock, both Daniel and Putnam survived the smallpox outbreak and blizzard. That spring, after gold was discovered in southern Oregon, the rush to the new mines drove traffic up the Columbia River and allowed Bradford and Company to make a full recovery. Demand for water transportation became so great that the Bradford brothers decided to re-attempt their

Clearing snow from railroad tracks in the Columbia Gorge. Winter storms like these shut down the OSN's operations for weeks. *Courtesy of Oregon Historical Society.*

steamboat venture. This time, Daniel minimized costs by commissioning a local shipwright to refurbish a wrecked sailboat, perform all the work above the rapids and use lumber from a local mill. The result was a larger, more powerful, more attractive and more comfortable side-wheeler, christened the *Mary*. The seventy-seven-foot-long, ninety-seven-ton *Mary* featured such amenities as a passenger cabin with a veranda and skylights.

Daniel expanded Bradford and Company by forming a partnership with a newly incorporated steamboat operator in Portland called the Columbia River Steam Navigation Company (CRSN). The partnership was a natural fit; Daniel had much in common with the CRSN's owner, Benjamin Stark. One of Portland's original Donation Land claimants, the Louisiana-born and raised Stark, unpopular in Portland because of his proslavery views and—much worse in the eyes of his associates—his bad credit, migrated west with the same goal as the Bradford brothers: to make quick profits and return east. Stark, who produced only mixed results from his many business ventures in Portland, founded the CRSN as yet another strategy

Western terminus of Bradford and Company portage tramway, near Fort Rains, Washington Territory. *Courtesy of Oregon Historical Society.*

to make his fortune on the frontier. Neither Stark nor the Bradfords had any affinity for steamboats, but the overwhelming demand for them on the Columbia River during the 1853 gold rush made them an attractive speculation strategy.

Bradford and Company and the CRSN combined to inaugurate the first full-service transportation line connecting Portland and The Dalles. The trip itinerary consisted of departure from Portland aboard the CRSN's steamboat, then a transfer to one of Bradford and Company's sailboats at settler George Johnson's Lower Cascades wharf, a second transfer from sailboat to the west terminus of the tramway and a mule-powered car ride to the Upper Cascades. Having taken a full day to get here, passengers passed the night at Bradford and Company's boardinghouse while freight was stored in a nearby warehouse. After breakfast the next morning, there was a third and final transfer to the *Mary*, which shipped passengers and freight to the end of the line at The Dalles by the afternoon. For the downriver journey, the process was reversed, the *Mary* departing The Dalles in the morning.

Daniel's new partnership proved highly profitable for Bradford and Company. A year after the service began, the brothers appeared to have reached their goal of achieving wealth and status on the western frontier. They enjoyed enough expendable income to build new houses, each with multiple bedrooms, a kitchen and large parlors for entertaining guests.

Putnam married a newly arrived settler, and Daniel presented her with the gift of a gold pocket watch. In a letter to her father back home, Putnam's wife described her satisfaction with the Bradfords' new lifestyle: "To tell the truth I have ev(e)ry thing that I want."

The Oregon Transportation Line

Reports about Bradford and Company's success at the Cascades spread throughout the region. The public complained about their exorbitant tramway tolls, but, because of a lack of viable alternatives, they were forced to pay any price. For the adventurous, optimistic and exceptionally risk-tolerant individual with resources—or the credit to borrow them at least—the problem presented an opportunity.

Joseph Ruckel was just such an individual. Like the Bradford brothers and Benjamin Stark, Ruckel migrated west to make his fortune from speculation. "Colonel" Ruckel, as he was affectionately referred by his friends and business associates in honor of his military service during the Mexican-American War, possessed a dynamic personality. Like Daniel, Ruckel was confident, persuasive and aggressive. Because of his investments in major transportation operations during his decade of residency in Oregon, Ruckel became something of a local celebrity in Portland. When Ruckel returned east in 1865, the *Oregon Weekly Times* praised him for his industrious, generous and exemplary character and lamented that he could "illy be spared from any community."

Away from the public gaze, Ruckel could be stubborn, vindictive and emotionally volatile. Early business partners complained of his unpredictable and explosive temper, paranoia and poor decision-making skills. A former employee once remembered Ruckel as "a good man, but a bad manager."

In 1855, after a stint as a San Francisco merchant, Ruckel moved to Oregon in search of a new adventure. He found it at the Cascades, where, on surveying Bradford and Company's operations across the river, he conceived a scheme to steal the Bradford brothers' customers by forming a competing transportation line.

Ruckel summoned his energy and industriousness to begin the herculean task of building a portage on the Oregon shore of the Cascades. His first step was to secure land, which he did by filing a claim for property across the river from today's Fort Rains. Ruckel's business partner, Harrison Olmstead, filed a claim directly west of Ruckel's. On both sides of their properties,

Joseph Ruckel's homestead and steamboat landing, directly across the river from Fort Rains, Washington Territory. *Courtesy of Oregon Historical Society.*

Ruckel and Olmstead obtained rights-of-way for the rest of their portage by entering into rental agreements with neighboring settlers. After control of the full six miles of Oregon shoreline at the Cascades was obtained, Ruckel and Olmstead hired a crew of laborers—some of them induced from Bradford and Company's employment—to begin clearing and grading for a wagon road. Ruckel and Olmstead filed incorporation paperwork for what they called the Oregon Transportation Line.

Next, Ruckel and Olmstead set up their steamboat service. For the route between the Cascades and The Dalles, they placed an order with Bradford and Company's builder, whose boatyard was conveniently located at the planned upriver terminus of the new portage. On the Cascades–Portland route, Ruckel and Olmstead formed a partnership with the new owners of Bradford and Company's wrecked *James P. Flint*, which since its sinking had been raised, patched and renamed *Fashion*.

By the summer of 1855, the Oregon Transportation Line was ready to receive customers. Ruckel and Olmstead's new steamboat, christened the *Wasco* after their new county of residence, transferred passengers and freight at a landing near the present site of the Cascade Locks Marina. The portage wagon road wound around the Oregon shore close to the water's edge, over trestles at Eagle Creek and Tooth Rock, and terminated at the *Fashion*'s landing, near the present site of the Bonneville Dam Navigation Lock.

Oregon portage at Middle Cascades. Strap-iron railroad is at left, abandoned trestle is at right. *Courtesy of Oregon Historical Society.*

The Oregon Transportation Line proved an immediate success. Most of the traffic passing through the Cascades diverted from the north to the south shore, as Ruckel and Olmstead's service was decidedly superior to that of Bradford and Company's; with only two transfers at the Cascades instead of Bradford and Company's three, an overnight layover was not necessary, which greatly increased the speed of a trip between Portland and The Dalles. Ruckel and Olmstead's *Wasco* became the obvious choice for travel, as it was twice the length and tonnage of Bradford and Company's *Mary* and more commodious.

The War between the Shores

Helplessly watching from across the river as Ruckel and Olmstead intercepted their customers and revenue, Daniel and Putnam realized their only chance to ensure their young company's survival was to win back their customers with superior facilities. To fund improvements, Daniel borrowed heavily, mortgaging his entire property at the Cascades in exchange for a line of credit from his cousin's firm in San Francisco.

Shortly after beginning renovations, the Bradford brothers suffered another, more literal attack on their business. Early one March morning in 1856, as a labor crew resumed their daily work renovating the tramway, a volley of gunfire rained down on the men from the ridge above. It was the initial assault of a three-day siege that would become famous in Pacific Northwest history as the Cascades Massacre, wherein a band of more than two hundred warriors from the Klickitat, Yakima and Cascades tribes launched a surprise attack on the Cascades settlement. Until U.S. Army troops arrived from Fort Vancouver and The Dalles to defend the area, most settlers barricaded themselves in the Bradford and Company store.

By the end of the massacre, the warriors had destroyed the company's lumber mill, wharf, warehouse and several tons of freight. Private residences were burned to the ground, including Putnam's new house. The *Mary* was riddled with bullet holes but escaped from its landing without serious damage. A total of seventeen Cascades settlers were killed, half of whom were on the Bradford and Company payroll. Several more were injured and could either no longer work or joined the many who moved out of Skamania County immediately following the incident.

After the attack, the Bradford brothers wasted no time in repairing their properties, lest Ruckel and Olmstead continue to drain their primary sources of income. Bradford and Company supervisor and massacre survivor Lawrence Coe reassured Putnam that the labor crew had resumed its progress within weeks of the carnage: "We have got to work again building and transporting; are going to build a sawmill as soon as we can." Meanwhile, Daniel invested in updating his steamboat line by placing an order to construct a larger, more powerful side-wheeler to replace the *Mary*. Meanwhile, Daniel's partner Benjamin Stark purchased a new and larger replacement for their steamboat servicing the route between Portland and the Cascades.

In 1857, Bradford and Company's new steamboats were launched, running and proving to be the new favorites on the river. The *Hassaloe*, serving the Cascades–The Dalles route, was decidedly faster and better appointed than the *Wasco*. The *Senorita*, cruising from Portland to the Cascades, was nearly twice the size of, faster and more comfortable than the *Fashion*. Ruckel and Olmstead's Oregon Transportation Line suddenly seemed outdated, underpowered and uncomfortable compared to Bradford and Company's new fleet. The brothers were relieved to witness the seasonal traffic flow return to their side of the river, and they reclaimed their dominance of Columbia River transportation.

Ruckel and Olmstead fumed at the sudden changes in their circumstances. They responded aggressively to claim an unchallengeable advantage. They took out large loans from a Portland bank and commissioned the construction of a new steamboat and a wooden tramway to be built over the wagon road from Eagle Creek to their steamboat landing downstream. Once completed, Ruckel and Olmstead's service would offer customers a tramway ride that circumnavigated the entire six miles of rapids at the Cascades. It would be the most comfortable and fastest means of travel between Portland and The Dalles.

At a loss for any viable competition strategy—and perhaps capital—Daniel approached Ruckel and Olmstead to discuss terms for a truce. Though the details of their conversation were not recorded, the result of the conference between the two sets of portage owners became known: with the leverage of a cash payment and an agreement to split future revenues, Daniel succeeded in convincing Ruckel and Olmstead to close their business, merge their newest steamboat with Bradford and Company's fleet, shut down their portage road and lay up their upriver steamboat. The arrangement allowed Bradford and Company to restore its monopoly of the Portland–The Dalles route and gain control of the best steamboats on the Columbia River.

It appeared that the war between the Cascades shores was over, but Ruckel and Olmstead would not remain satisfied with peace terms for long.

2

UNION

The year 1859 started painfully for Captain John Ainsworth.

The previous summer had been rewarding—emotionally, professionally and financially. Ainsworth joined the masses in their flock to the Fraser River, where, instead of taking his place among the prospectors panning for gold in the gravelly riverbed, he transported them to the mining sites, making history as the first to navigate the upper reaches of the Fraser on a steamboat. It was a magical time for Ainsworth, one that created romantic memories that he enjoyed for the rest of his life. "The sensation to me," Ainsworth mused decades later, "of entering a water that had never before been divided by the prow of a Steamer is beyond description."

By autumn, the Fraser River rush was over and Ainsworth was back in Portland. Though the local economy was sluggish, Ainsworth had employment as captain of the steamboat *Carrie Ladd*. This vessel, the second stern-wheeler built in the Pacific Northwest, was also the second designed, owned and operated by Ainsworth and his business partner, Jacob Kamm.

Ainsworth met Kamm, a Swedish immigrant, when the two began their careers in steam navigation on the Mississippi River during the 1840s. As young men in their twenties, they bonded over their passion for steamboats and their common career goals of climbing the crew ranks; Ainsworth aspired to be a captain, while Kamm dreamed of commanding an engine room. Both followed their peers west after news of the California gold rush

Left: John Ainsworth, 1864. Ainsworth was founder and president of the OSN. *Courtesy of Oregon Historical Society*.

Right: Jacob Kamm, founder, chief engineer and major stockholder of the OSN. *Courtesy of Oregon Historical Society*.

reached the South. They reunited later in Sacramento City, where they were hired by an Oregon investor to operate the side-wheeler *Lot Whitcomb*.

The *Carrie Ladd*'s business produced impressive returns for Ainsworth, Kamm and their partners, paying the men over $7,000 in dividends in 1859 alone. But Ainsworth had paid an enormous price for this success. By the beginning of that year, Ainsworth had become overwhelmed, exhausted and even depressed with the demands of being an owner-operator with a small crew. Snow, ice and gale-force winds in the Columbia Gorge the previous winter had made for harrowing trips. Staffing problems, including the illness of the purser and the accidental drowning of the cook, forced Ainsworth to put in many additional and stressful hours filling in until suitable replacements could be hired. "I have felt to day thuroughly disgusted with *everything*," Ainsworth scribbled in his diary at the end of a long day in February, "would be glad to sell out and leave a country that I have lost all affection for."

Ainsworth contemplated his escape from the hectic daily grind of the entrepreneurial lifestyle and itched for a new adventure. As was his practice when considering most major life decisions, he consulted his close friend and business partner, Robert Thompson.

ROBERT THOMPSON

Thompson was one of the few men who had made a fortune from panning gold during the initial rush to California in 1848. He was also one of the even fewer who spent that fortune wisely. Thompson's thirty-year business career in Oregon serves as a lesson in the compounding power of conservative, concentrated, thoughtful and timely investment decisions. After striking gold, Thompson sailed north and settled in Oregon City, where he purchased interests in lumber and gristmills. A few years later, Thompson sold his mill equity and purchased a large flock of sheep, which he drove around the Cascade Mountains to his new home at The Dalles. Here, Thompson started a livestock business and, thanks to his political connections and financial support of Franklin Pierce's presidential campaign, was offered a job as the U.S. government's liaison to Native American tribes in the eastern section of the Oregon territory.

Robert Thompson, 1863. Thompson helped found the OSN and was Ainsworth's closest friend and business partner. *Author's collection.*

Thompson met Ainsworth at the Oregon City Masonic lodge shortly after the two men arrived in the Northwest. After learning that Ainsworth was broke—his employer refused to pay him until the steamboat on which he was hired was finished with construction—Thompson agreed to cover Ainsworth's living expenses until he received his first salary payment.

The gesture marked the beginning of an inseparable friendship that lasted forty-three years, until Ainsworth's death in 1893. Though the two men differed on such major worldviews as politics and religion—Thompson was a highly active Democrat and devoutly religious, while Ainsworth remained passively Republican and resentful of religious institutions—they enjoyed a rewarding relationship based on deep mutual respect and affection. Of their twenty years together co-managing the OSN, Ainsworth recalled that he and Thompson "worked almost as one man in forming and carrying out the different policies of the company." Reflecting on his feelings for his friend, Thompson wrote of how much he was touched by Ainsworth's integrity: "I know him for a good and just man…and a humane man….I do not know his superior. He is one of God's noblemen." Both men fed off each other's management philosophies, methodical thinking and long-range visions for the future, but the unshakeable foundation of Ainsworth and Thompson's bond was based on their seemingly inexhaustible source of energy and the sharing of a common goal: the advancement of their business interests.

THE SECRET WEAPON

In 1859, Ainsworth and Thompson concluded that it was time to put into action an idea that they had been discussing for several years: the consolidation of all Willamette and Columbia steamboat companies.

In addition to Ainsworth's personal motives for reviving the idea, other circumstances converged to render timing especially opportune. Prevailing economic conditions made competition particularly intense, driving up overhead costs for steamboat owners. Consequently, relations between the Cascades portage owners were now worse than ever. Ruckel and Olmstead reneged on their agreement with the Bradfords, took back their steamboats and reopened their transportation line. When Ainsworth surveyed the situation at the Cascades, he found the mood "very inharmonious," concluding that the portage owners "had little confidence in each other." Ainsworth noted that the reopening of Ruckel and Olmstead's line and its subsequent rapid encroachment on Bradford and Company's business caused Daniel and Putnam to harbor "much disgust and jealousy" for their competitors across the river.

Perhaps the most significant reason why 1859 appeared to Ainsworth and Thompson the best time to consolidate was the leverage Ainsworth possessed that year in a secret weapon he had at his disposal: the *Carrie Ladd*. This unassuming stern-wheeler, though small, was the most powerful steamboat yet seen on the Columbia River and broke records on every route it cruised. Ainsworth was convinced that the *Carrie Ladd* was powerful enough to accomplish what no steamboat had done before: scale the Lower Cascades rapids.

To affect a consolidation, Ainsworth visited each Columbia River steamboat owner and asked them to join him in his mission. Ainsworth first met with Benjamin Stark, explaining that at the wheel of the *Carrie Ladd*, he was sure he could make regular trips between Portland and Fort Rains, a point on the Washington shoreline just above the Lower Cascade rapids. Stark understood that if Ainsworth was correct, his steamboat would set

Stern-wheeler *Cascade* at the OSN's floating wharf and railroad terminus at Lower Cascades. *Courtesy of Oregon Historical Society.*

a new precedent on the Portland–The Dalles route that would not only prove much faster than Stark's existing service but also surpass Ruckel and Olmstead's line in speed. More important for the profit-hungry Stark was the fact that, if he added the *Carrie Ladd* to his fleet, and she could reach Fort Rains reliably, the Lower Cascades wharf and sailboat service would be rendered redundant. Stark could then eliminate the owner of the Lower Cascades operation from his business agreement and absorb their cut of revenue, doubling Stark's profit.

Stark accepted Ainsworth's proposition to consolidate, and the *Carrie Ladd* immediately began making trips to the Cascades. Ainsworth knew his vessel well; she made Fort Rains without incident. Ruckel and Olmstead watched helplessly across the river as the stout steamer chugged past the first two miles of their portage.

Ruckel and Olmstead quickly realized that they could not compete with the *Carrie Ladd*, or, as Ainsworth described it, they "felt the crushing effect of my boat." Already deep in debt with their Portland bankers, to continue running their transportation line on their own would likely require incurring even more debt to fund continued improvements, repairs and a likely need to cover losses. Convinced they were now out of options, Ruckel and Olmstead decided to admit defeat. They approached Ainsworth and Stark with a proposal to join their partnership in exchange for their best steamboat. Ainsworth and Stark accepted.

Having successfully consolidated all steamboat companies below the Cascades, Ainsworth filed incorporation paperwork in the Washington territory for what he called the Union Transportation Company, which made history as the largest shipping company yet formed in the Pacific Northwest. But before Ainsworth and Thompson's vision for a true consolidation could be realized, more history had to be made.

3

THE FIRST GUN

The original arrangement of the Union Transportation Company appeared mutually beneficial to all involved. With competition eliminated, a monopoly was created, and the partners charged rates as high as the market would bear. Ruckel and Olmstead were allowed to retain ownership of their tramway, which would serve as a backup portage in the event that the *Carrie Ladd* could not reach Fort Rains or the Bradford and Company tramway was inoperable.

But Ainsworth and Thompson were not satisfied. Their vision was to consolidate all steamboat owners on the Columbia River, not just those operating below the Cascades. The *Hassalo* was in 1859 the only steamboat that provided service between the Cascades and The Dalles, allowing its owner, Bradford and Company, their own monopoly over that critical stretch of river. Ainsworth was determined to absorb this monopoly into Union's, adding another source of revenue and an additional forty-five miles of service area. To accomplish this, Ainsworth needed to both convince Daniel and Putnam Bradford to join Union and facilitate a new revenue-sharing agreement among all parties.

Accomplishing this task required Ainsworth to lead the most grueling negotiation of his career. "The difficulties I had to encounter," Ainsworth wrote years later of the affair, "were *very much greater* than I can possibly make you understand." Even when, at length, an agreement was reached between all parties, Ainsworth acknowledged that the negotiation ultimately served as "the first gun to a battle that waged hot and long" among Union's partners for the next several years.

Ruckel and Olmstead versus the Bradfords

From the time Ruckel and Olmstead established their claims at the Cascades, their relationship with the Bradford brothers had grown increasingly contentious. For nearly four years, jealousy, resentment, contempt and anxiety hung heavy in the air over the rapids, as the owners on each side of the river exhausted their financial and physical resources attempting to outdo each other. The men's failure to cooperate as co-managers, and Ruckel and Olmstead's recent breaking of their truce with the Bradfords, made the situation worse.

Bringing the portage owners together to sit in the same room was its own feat that required the marshaling of Ainsworth's most effective persuasion skills to accomplish. The feuding men could no longer avoid one another and privately nurse their negative thoughts and feelings. Ainsworth forced them to confront their differences. He saw no way around it if Union was to survive.

The tension in the room where the portage owners met was palpable when Ainsworth began the negotiation. There was a heavy mood that Ainsworth remembered years later he could both "see and feel." After a long discussion, Ainsworth was successful in convincing the Bradford brothers to join Union, but the brothers were highly cautious, as their incentive was negligible. Consolidation allowed the brothers to increase their income by claiming a share of revenue from other sources, but in doing so, they were forced to relinquish control of their business and forfeit their monopoly over a forty-five-mile stretch of the Columbia River. To make matters more precarious, consolidation meant that the Bradfords would be forced to work alongside their former nemeses, Ruckel and Olmstead.

When the discussion turned to the complicated task of establishing a cash value for each steamboat under Union's control, the proceedings imploded. The portage owners could no longer contain themselves. Emotions escalated, accusations were made and insults were exchanged. Both Ruckel and Daniel Bradford threatened to rescind their involvement with the partners and compete with Union and undercut the consolidation's freight and passenger rates until the new company was financially ruined by operating losses. Ironically—because he possessed the least means to act on them compared to the rest of the Union partners—it was the blustering, short-tempered Ruckel who made the most outlandish threats. Ainsworth tried his best to mediate what he described as a "war of words," but it was to no avail. With difficulty, he interrupted the shouting match and adjourned the meeting in exasperation.

Ainsworth allowed the portage owners time to soothe themselves and then called them together again to re-initiate negotiations. Another impasse occurred, shouting ensued and threats were exchanged. Ainsworth was once again forced to prematurely shut down the meeting after another "row" broke out between Ruckel and Daniel.

Ainsworth attempted to resume negotiations on several more occasions over a period of several weeks, and in each instance, the same result occurred. It appeared as if Union was destined to fail. The portage owners seemed incapable of putting aside their differences, prioritizing the company's interests over their own or controlling their emotions. After several weeks of volatility that deepened the rift between the portage owners and increased Ainsworth's frustrations with them, the group finally agreed on a valuation for each steamboat and split the equity in the business among all partners. With the inclusion of the Bradford brothers and their assets, Union extended its monopoly from the Cascades to The Dalles.

Though it took a massive effort to get this far, Ainsworth still sought more control over the Columbia River. There was one final step necessary to attain the vision that he and Thompson had discussed at length: to bring Thompson himself into the Union partnership.

THE PORTAGE OWNERS VERSUS THOMPSON

Ironically, though he and Ainsworth had for years shared the same vision of consolidation, by 1859, Thompson was the steamboat owner least likely to join Union.

In business, Thompson was doing well enough on his own. Soon after moving to The Dalles and starting his government job, the restless Thompson began dabbling in transportation and partnered with the owner of a portage road bypassing the unnavigable Celilo Falls. Thompson then invested in the construction of a fleet of sailboats at the eastern terminus of the portage and made history with the first river transportation service above The Dalles. Thompson and his partners remained unchallenged throughout the second half of the 1850s and enjoyed the benefits of a monopoly in high demand. They charged high rates and, thanks to Thompson's government connections, secured lucrative contracts to ship U.S. Army troops and materials up the Columbia River during the Yakima War. The business was

Celilo Falls, an ancient Native American fishery and previously unnavigable section of the Columbia River, now inundated by The Dalles Dam. *Courtesy of Oregon Historical Society.*

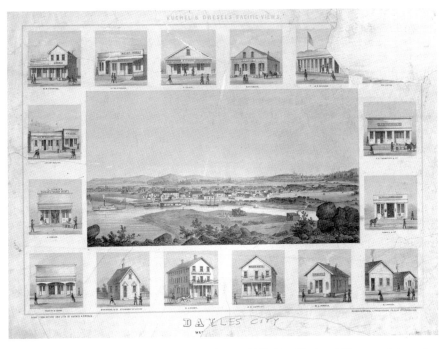

The Dalles and its prominent business proprietors, 1859. Bradford and Company's branch office and Thompson's mercantile are listed. *Courtesy of Oregon Historical Society.*

generating such enormous profits that Thompson quit his government job, mercantile firm and farm and invested all his resources into the expansion of his transportation empire. In 1858, Thompson commissioned the construction of the first steamboat in history to operate above The Dalles, which quickly became the most profitable aspect of his transportation service. When Union was formed in 1859, Thompson was at the height of his business success.

Besides forfeiting his lucrative business and a portion of its profits, if Thompson were to join Union, he would be forced to work alongside his longtime opponents, the Cascades portage owners. The tension between Thompson and the portage owners began in 1857, when Lawrence Coe, then working for Bradford and Company as manager, suddenly resigned to partner with Thompson. With the help of Coe's inside knowledge of business at the Cascades, Thompson and Coe attempted to extend Thompson's transportation line to the Cascades by constructing a steamboat to compete with those owned by the portage owners. The steamboat wrecked at the beginning of its maiden voyage, but Thompson promptly repaired it and sent it up the Fraser River, where the steamboat arrived in time to profit handsomely from the gold rush. The Bradford brothers attempted to compete with Thompson by sending their own steamboat up the Fraser, but the scheme failed and saddled Bradford and Company with a loss of their investment and an extra steamboat they failed to charter profitably.

When Ainsworth proposed to the Union partners that they bring in Thompson, the group's response triggered another crisis. The portage owners protested loudly. They groaned at the prospect of partnering with a former opponent and were convinced that Thompson would balk at the idea of sharing his empire. Even if Thompson were to be willing to join Union, the portage owners rationalized, he would likely demand unreasonable terms. As usual, Ruckel reacted with the most emotion, protested with the most hostility and threatened to withdraw his steamboats and compete with Union if Ainsworth approached Thompson about joining the combine. Leveraging his gifts of persuasion, Ainsworth was able to pacify Ruckel and the other portage owners with personal testimonies of Thompson's character and a reassurance that Thompson shared the same vision for consolidation as the Union partners.

Ainsworth's appeals proved successful. He not only convinced the group to allow Thompson to join Union but also obtained approval to pay him $18,000 in cash or equity to properly incentivize the absorption of his assets. The partners traveled to The Dalles to personally present their offer to Thompson. They were floored when Thompson amicably accepted and agreed with the group's consensus on their estimated value of his steamboat.

Then, the righteous and prideful Thompson changed his tone and delivered a sobering harangue to the Cascades portage owners. In what Ainsworth later described as an "exacting" manner, Thompson informed them that he had heard about their attacks on his character, that their accusations were false and that he would not tolerate any more slander.

By April 1859, Ainsworth had succeeded in consolidating every Columbia River steamboat operation into a single entity. After Thompson joined, Union claimed ownership of nine steamboats servicing an area of more than three hundred river miles. The new company recorded its capital as $172,500, the sum of the valuations that the partners had argued long and hard to assign each of their steamboats.

What was once just an amusing topic of conversation between Ainsworth and Thompson was now a reality. After facing much more difficulty than he ever thought possible in coaxing a small group of men to cooperate with one another, the consolidation was now contractually and logistically positioned to thrive on its own as a monopoly. Each partner could now enjoy regular residual income from their split of Union's revenue.

Ainsworth's work, however, was far from over.

4

INCORPORATION

U nion secured its partnership with Thompson in time to capitalize on the seasonal increase in upper Columbia River traffic. Thompson's steamboat, the small but powerful *Colonel Wright*, began making trips farther up the Snake River than she had ever ventured before. On one eastbound trip, she ascended the river fifty miles, and on a westbound trip, she broke the record from Walla Walla to Portland, finishing the run in just thirty hours.

Union was making both history and revenue with its steamboats, but a nagging concern became difficult for Ainsworth to ignore: though the portages at The Dalles and the Cascades were the most critical links in Union's transportation chain, the company possessed virtually no effective control over them. Shared revenue agreements, ownership and valuation of Union's assets pertained exclusively to its steamboat fleet, leaving control of the three portages to their respective owners. Such autonomy allowed each portage owner discretion to ship whatever freight and passengers they wished—including those of Union's competitors—undermining the new company's monopoly and increasing opportunities for competition. Compounding the threat of the portages to Union was the ongoing rivalry among Ruckel, Olmstead and the Bradford brothers, which continued to energize the dynamic of resentment, anxiety, jealousy, paranoia and distrust that persisted both in and outside of Union's meetings.

MARSHALLING RESOURCES

Ainsworth realized that such a lack of control over the portages called for a closer, more powerful and better organized arrangement.

In the spring of 1860, he made aggressive moves toward this end. First, with Thompson, Ruckel and Daniel, Ainsworth drafted and submitted to the Washington territorial legislature a petition to re-incorporate Union under a new name, the Oregon Steam Navigation Company. In the document, the partners included broad language to account for future expansion. They wrote that OSN was being organized "for the purposes of navigation and Transportation in the State of Oregon and Washington Territory.... Said Corporation Shall have power to purchase and receive...lands, goods, Chattels, and effects of every kind." Also in the document, the partners outlined a plan to monetize each steamboat owner's allotted portion of company equity by issuing two thousand shares of company stock, each with an assigned par value of $500, totaling $1 million in capital.

Orlando Humason, Thompson's transportation business partner at The Dalles. The OSN purchased Humason's portage and replaced it with a railroad. *Courtesy of Oregon State University.*

Next, Ainsworth set out to increase the new organization's influence over the portages, the most critical links in the transportation line. He initiated discussions with every portage owner for the purpose of negotiating subsidy contracts to transport OSN freight exclusively. Ainsworth's meeting with Orlando Humason, Thompson's longtime partner and owner of The Dalles portage, was brief. Humason quickly agreed to ship only OSN freight in exchange for a subsidy of twenty dollars per ton of government freight and fifteen dollars per ton of civilian freight.

Unlike his brief talk with Humason, Ainsworth's negotiations with the Cascades portage owners dragged painfully on for several months. As usual, there was much bickering, many emotional outbursts, demands and accusations. After nearly half a year, Ainsworth and the portage owners finally reached a heavily nuanced agreement. The contract featured many stipulations, including that Ruckel and Olmstead be allowed to ship freight by any customer they desired from their portage terminus below the Cascades to the steamboat landing at the middle rapid and that even though signatures were not affixed to the contract until October, it be backdated to May 1860. As compensation, the portage owners agreed to split 25 percent—Bradford and Company to keep 58.3 percent of this portion, Ruckel and Olmstead to keep the balance—of OSN revenue from any freight, specie and mail shipped between Portland and The Dalles.

The Oregon Steam Navigation Company Is Born

After six months at Olympia, the petition for the OSN's incorporation was approved in an act of the Washington territorial legislature. The company charter was granted with the stipulation that the company's fleet of steamboats be registered in Washington and subjected to the territory's property tax.

Just a few days after notice arrived from Olympia, the former Union partners met in Vancouver to finish setting up their new company. In attendance at the meeting were many new faces, formerly distant and uninvolved members of the original partnership, now possessing a serious energy about the opportunities at hand in the Washington territory's largest business operation. Among these new attendees were Simeon Reed and the Ladd brothers, William and John.

Simeon Reed's connections with the OSN were through Stark's Columbia River Steam Navigation Company, which Reed joined as a speculation scheme. Reed, who had just turned thirty years of age, was the youngest member of the OSN leadership team. Tall, muscular, with brooding eyes and a bushy beard, Reed was often the center of attention at social gatherings because of his flashy image; namely, his bold dress, genial manners and expensive tastes in bourbon, wine and cigars. Reed came west in 1851 and established himself in Sacramento, where he sold lumber and flour to gold prospectors out of a tent. In 1853, after losing almost everything they owned in a fire, Reed and his wife sailed for Oregon. After two years scraping by as a frontier merchant on the lower Columbia River, Reed moved to Portland and accepted a job as a clerk in the general store of William Ladd. William eventually sold his store to his brother John and Reed. By the time Union was formed, Reed had become wealthy through profitable investments in the store and, most recently, Columbia River steamboats.

The OSN's first official meeting was on December 29, 1860. The attendees spent the afternoon drafting a company constitution, which outlined the

William Ladd mansion, at the corner of Southwest Broadway and Jefferson Streets, Portland. *Courtesy of Oregon Historical Society.*

Left: Simeon Reed, early 1870s. Reed was at the height of his career at the OSN when this photo was taken. *Courtesy of Oregon Historical Society.*

Right: William Ladd, banker, board member and stockholder of the OSN. *Courtesy of Oregon Historical Society.*

Joseph Bailey and family, 1867. Bailey managed the Oregon portage and was one of the original OSN shareholders. *Courtesy of Oregon Historical Society.*

decisions the men made that day in creating bureaucratic procedures to be recognized by company stockholders and officers. The group voted on the creation of a board of directors, which would assume the responsibility of making the organization's most important management decisions. Three officer positions were created, including a president, vice-president and secretary, to be elected by the board. There would be at least one stockholder and board meeting each year, with the board granted the option to meet on a monthly basis, or more often if requested by the president. The company secretary was assigned the responsibility of preparing an annual report of the financial status and performance of the business over the previous year, which would be read aloud and discussed by board members during each annual meeting.

After resolving to adopt their constitution, the meeting attendees applied their new procedures to practice by holding an election to create the first OSN Board of Directors. Ainsworth, Daniel Bradford, Ruckel, Reed and Lawrence Coe were nominated and elected. Before the close of the meeting, Coe, another speculation-minded former confidant of the Bradford brothers, proposed that the capital stock of the newly formed company be tripled to $517,500. Coe's motion was accepted by the group, granting each stockholder two additional shares per existing share and increasing the value of their original investment by 200 percent.

The Dalles waterfront, 1867. OSN railroad terminus, wharf, warehouse and machine shop are at right. *Courtesy of Oregon Historical Society.*

The OSN Board of Directors held their first meeting a few days later. First on the agenda was the election of company officers, which resulted in Ainsworth as president, Daniel as vice-president and Bradford and Company partner George Murray as secretary. The group also elected Coe to serve as agent to manage OSN operations at The Dalles and Jacob Kamm as chief engineer of the OSN's fleet.

What was once a loose partnership of steamboat owners was now a large-scale, modern and capitalistic corporation, the first of its kind in the Pacific Northwest. In adding new and lucrative service areas and paying portage owners to refuse their services to competitors, Ainsworth secured the power of the OSN's monopoly of Columbia River transportation. Leadership, decision-making and equity were now clearly defined and structured to function as an efficient system, rewarding ownership, responsibility and trust within the organization. The processes, procedures and organization of the OSN were specifically designed with the flexibility necessary to keep pace with growth, at least as far as the new board of directors could forecast it.

5

THE FIRST RUSH

During the same winter the OSN was incorporated, a small party of prospectors rode deep into the newly established Nez Perce reservation, made camp along the banks of Orofino Creek and uncovered a large amount of gold in its bed. Though with the Treaty of Walla Walla the U.S. government promised to allot this creek and millions of acres around it exclusively to the Nez Perce tribe, the government did not discourage the rampant trespassing that ensued after word of the Orofino Creek gold strike spread throughout the country.

By April 1861, the rush to the Nez Perce reservation was in full swing. Gold seekers and the opportunists who sought to make money off them left the picked-through lodes of California and British Columbia and flocked to the untapped lands of the eastern Washington Territory. Speed and the safety of their cargo were the highest priorities for those traveling to Orofino Creek. Their best chances at both were to follow the Columbia, Snake and Clearwater Rivers, the only communication with one of the remotest corners of the Northwest frontier, situated 150 miles from the Columbia and twice as far from The Dalles, the last substantial settlement east of Portland.

For those who had faith in the promise of the latest American El Dorado, the OSN's multimodal transportation system was the obvious choice of conveyance to the diggings. A prospector could disembark from their ocean passage at Astoria and be transported five hundred miles to Lewiston, all by the OSN and its contractors. A few months into the rush, steamboat service had extended as far inland as Slaterville, a tent community that

The Dalles street scene, during the gold rush of 1864. *Courtesy of Oregon State University.*

sprang up on the shores of the Clearwater River. Here, prospectors could purchase animals to complete the last leg of their journey to the Nez Perce reservation. Thankfully, for both the OSN and the throngs scrambling to the new mines, the OSN's services and management structure were functional when the rush began.

The 1861 gold rush tested the durability of that structure to a degree that none of the directors had ever imagined. Where there were once too many steamboats competing for too few customers, now passengers and shippers were fighting for passage aboard what proved to be far too few vessels, powered by steam or sail.

THE BOTTLENECK

The OSN's steamboats struggled to keep up with the sudden and dramatic influx in traffic, but the more immediate problem was the transfer at the Cascades. The logistical challenges of portaging overland around the rapids caused a breakdown in the OSN's system, and the management styles of the portage owners made the situation worse. By April, the problem had turned into a crisis.

Just when Ruckel and Olmstead's tramway was needed most, it was rendered inoperable. Spring flooding tore away trestles, causing extensive damage. Repairs took several months to execute and thousands of dollars to fund. In the meantime, the tramway was impassable, and patrons were turned away.

All traffic was diverted to the Washington side of the river, which compounded another major problem. Freight arrived at Bradford and Company's tramway termini at a faster rate than it could be processed and shipped, filling up warehouses beyond capacity. With nowhere to store it securely, Bradford and Company employees were forced to stack freight along the tramway as it awaited shipment. As the busy days wore on, rows of stacked freight grew along the tramway until it spanned the entire one and a half miles to the opposite terminus.

Daniel ordered extra steamboat trips to the Cascades and wagons and teams to help relieve the backlog. "It will not answer to allow the freight to accumulate," Daniel cried in a hasty note to Lawrence Coe, in charge of logistics at The Dalles. "Use every exertion…so there may be as little delay as possible." Untold tons of material arrived at the termini and were never shipped; they were misplaced, damaged or sent back to their owners. Bradford and Company neglected to invest in any effective security measures to protect the freight, and theft became an increasing problem.

The OSN constructed these living quarters for its managers at The Dalles. *Courtesy of Oregon Historical Society.*

At OSN headquarters in Vancouver, Ainsworth could do little more about the freight losses than field reports from various employees about what they claimed they witnessed, pass these on to the portage owners and appeal to them to act. Inevitably, losses began to accumulate. In a single month, the OSN was forced to pay over $10,000 to settle claims submitted by shippers. Ainsworth fumed. The OSN was losing precious profit and reputation, both critical for the first few months of a new company, and it was all because of mismanagement of property that he was powerless to change.

The amount of labor required during the gold rush of 1861, in Ainsworth's words, "greatly overtaxed" the OSN employees. "I scarcely have time to eat," he wrote a friend during the height of the busy season, "and everyone connected with the company is hurried as much." The workload proved too much for Lawrence Coe, who resigned at the end of the year.

Payday

Despite huge claim payments and a logistical nightmare at the Cascades, the OSN board was surprised by another completely unexpected phenomenon during their first year of business: enormous profits. Thanks particularly to the high rates the company charged for passage above The Dalles and their method of determining freight tonnage not by weight but by spatial measurement—wagons were measured by adding length with the tongue fully extended horizontally and height with the tongue fully extended vertically—the company's performance, as Ainsworth described it, "exceeded our most sanguine expectations." The OSN had so much surplus cash by summer that the board members decided to reward themselves for their hard work. During their June meeting, the board passed a motion to issue each stockholder one additional share per existing share, increasing the capital of the company by 35 percent, for a new total of $690,000. A few months later, the board increased its capital stock again, this time by 40 percent, for a new total of $966,000. In addition to issuing these new shares, the board began making dividend payments to stockholders and, by the end of the year, had paid shareholders a total of 10 percent of the par value of their shares.

As the Civil War gained momentum on the East Coast and the nation reeled after losing more than four thousand of its young men at Bull Run, OSN stockholders enjoyed a 470 percent increase in the value of their shares and looked forward to another profitable year ahead. There was every

OSN stock certificate, signed by Ainsworth, Thompson and Theodore Wygant, company secretary. These shares were once owned by Jay Cooke. *Author's collection.*

indication that another rush to the Orofino mines would be on in the coming spring, as large amounts of gold continued to be shipped downriver on the company's steamboats into the late fall. Prospects for the next year appeared even better when Ainsworth secured a major contract for the OSN to carry the U.S. Mail from the eastern terminus of the portage at The Dalles to Walla Walla at a rate of fifty dollars per trip. To prepare for the crowds clamoring upriver during the coming busy season, the board approved the construction of larger, more powerful and more commodious steamboats to service the route above The Dalles.

Amid the triumphant and optimistic moods of the board meetings, Ainsworth privately grappled with internal turmoil. He had grown increasingly focused on a major problem within the OSN that had existed long before its inception. The pressure applied to the OSN during its first year of business exposed the true severity and urgency of this issue and its alarming implications for the company's supposedly bright future. Now, Ainsworth was convinced more than ever that if this problem wasn't resolved before the next seasonal increase in traffic, the OSN could not succeed.

6

THE MISSING LINKS

Years after their private consultations in 1861, Ainsworth recalled that in his early discussions with Thompson about their new company, the two men concluded with certitude that "the O.S.N. Co. *must* control the Portages or the Portages *must* control and swallow up the Comp'y."

The system breakdown at the Cascades cost the OSN tens of thousands of dollars in damage claim payments and sullied the fragile reputation that the new company was attempting to establish. With the Cascades portages still in the hands of their original owners and the prospect of another year of overwhelming traffic ahead, the problem seemed likely to worsen.

Ainsworth and Thompson realized that a significant contributing factor to the problem was a lack of facilities at the portages. Though the tramways were a marked improvement over a bumpy wagon trail, they were subject to other vagaries, such as low speed of passage, unpredictable delays, frequent repairs and long periods of shutdown due to persistent environmental hazards. In order to minimize such incumbrances in the future, Ainsworth and Thompson could see that the most practical means of conveyance around the Cascades rapids was by a modern railroad, complete with iron rails, steam locomotives and enclosed cars.

More so than the tramways and environmental hazards, Ainsworth and Thompson were convinced that the most significant liability presented by the Cascades portages was their current management. Though it was obvious to Ainsworth and Thompson that Ruckel, Olmstead and the Bradford brothers remained so hyper-focused on their portages that "all of their actions, both in and out" of the OSN, were "governed by" them, their motivation was ultimately misplaced: the portage owners were less interested in providing quality service to their customers and more interested in dominating one another, or, as Ainsworth put it, "each ready and willing to annihilate the other should a favorable opportunity present itself."

Ironically, late in 1861, both Ruckel and Daniel made plans to construct their own steam-powered railroads over the portages. Ruckel ordered a small locomotive from a firm on the East Coast and Daniel purchased rights-of-way across his neighbors' properties for the construction of tracks. But Ainsworth and Thompson agreed that neither Ruckel nor Daniel possessed the management skills or ability to raise the large amounts of capital necessary to complete such large projects. Both portage owners were already deep in debt and valued fast and cheap construction over quality, safety and durability. "I mean to spend as little as possible on repairs," Daniel once admitted to Thompson in a private letter. "Let your property if necessity does not demand repairs depreciate."

AINSWORTH AND THOMPSON'S SECRET PLAN

Though the concept of Ainsworth and Thompson's goal to gain control of the Cascades portages was simple, achieving it seemed impossible. Most inconvenient for Ainsworth and Thompson was the fact that after the lucrative season of 1861, Ruckel, Olmstead and the Bradford brothers were less inclined than ever to give up control of their portages. Furthermore, now that their contract for OSN subsidies was effective, the portage owners looked forward to four more years of steady monthly payments. Meanwhile, the owners avoided the expense of settling claims filed by shippers for any lost, stolen or damaged freight that occurred at their portages, as the owners were not liable for property belonging to OSN customers.

In order to gain control at the Cascades, Ainsworth and Thompson needed to convince Olmstead and Daniel, deed holders, to sell all their portage assets to the OSN. Ainsworth and Thompson agreed that their best strategy for doing so was to appeal to the portage owners' primary motivation: making quick profits, minimizing expenses and, above all, outdoing one another. Ainsworth and Thompson understood that the portage owners' anxiety, though disruptive during OSN meetings, was energy that could be harnessed to drive them to sell.

Ainsworth wrote later that the crux of his and Thompson's plan was to "pull the right strings" with the portage owners and manipulate them to sell their portages. Ainsworth, who had a history of duping business associates whom he felt lacked integrity or had attempted to take advantage of him, took pleasure in working with his close friend to outsmart the portage owners. Ainsworth mused that he and Thompson "saw before us the necessity of playing the part of Good generals," strategizing to achieve victory in a symbolic battle.

Ainsworth and Thompson would be required to summon their best persuasion and deception skills to execute a detailed, lengthy and time-sensitive ruse while maintaining strict secrecy and much flexibility of their normally high moral standards. It was a particularly risky undertaking, since Bradford and Company, being the largest OSN stockholder (19 percent of all outstanding shares), enjoyed proportional voting power and, as such, a substantial amount of influence over OSN policy. Ainsworth and Thompson knew that if their plan failed and Daniel was provoked, he would likely indulge in his vindictive disposition and vote, along with his supporters on the board, to oppose Ainsworth and Thompson's goals, even restrict their power.

Taking the Washington Shore

Ainsworth and Thompson's first maneuver to secure the Cascades portages was to apply indirect pressure on the owners to sell, with the introduction of company policy supporting their agenda. At a meeting in December 1861, Ainsworth and Thompson easily convinced the board to agree that the OSN should purchase the portage at The Dalles. Absorbing this property, which would eliminate the expense of paying the current owner monthly freight subsidies and allow the OSN to employ more wagons and animals to ship freight over the portage and at a faster rate, appeared to all board members a necessary strategy.

At the next board meeting, Ainsworth and Thompson proposed the construction of a steam-powered railroad connecting The Dalles and Celilo, where the OSN owned a wharf, warehouses and a shipyard. Because of the high cost of construction and of purchasing rolling stock and other equipment, several board members were hesitant. The parsimonious Cascades portage owners were vehemently opposed, especially Ruckel and Olmstead. Ainsworth and Thompson addressed the portage owners' concerns

Left: The *D.F. Bradford* was one of the two original 4-2-4 tank locomotives ordered by the OSN to inaugurate its first railroad service at the Cascades. *Courtesy of Oregon Historical Society.*

Opposite: The first steam locomotive to operate in the Pacific Northwest, dubbed "The Pony," was purchased by Ruckel and Olmstead for their portage railroad in 1862. *Courtesy of Oregon Historical Society.*

by arguing that the completion of the proposed railroad would increase the value of their property at the Cascades. Ruckel and Olmstead persisted in their objections, but Daniel became immediately attached to the prospect of selling his portage at a higher price once the railroad was completed. True to his speculative agenda, Daniel could not resist an opportunity to make a quick profit and supplied the vote that carried the approval of the railroad's construction. Outvoted, Ruckel and Olmstead were now powerless to stop the project and were so disgusted that they refused to attend the next several board meetings.

After traffic picked up again in the spring of 1862, the Bradford brothers grew increasingly distressed as they again began to lose customers to Ruckel and Olmstead. During annual spring flooding in April, the *Carrie Ladd* was experiencing increasing difficulty in overcoming the rising water at the Cascades. It was clear that soon, the Washington portage would be unreachable by any vessel until the flood receded. Traffic began to divert to the Oregon portage, where steamboats could still reach the downriver terminus below the rapids. The Bradfords helplessly looked on as their business volume dwindled.

At the end of April, the brothers panicked when they encountered another, more permanent threat to their business. At Ruckel and Olmstead's wharf below the Cascades, Daniel and Putnam witnessed a steam locomotive being unloaded from a barge. Their tracks nearly complete, Ruckel and

Olmstead would soon inaugurate the first modern railroad service in the Pacific Northwest and render their portage faster and more reliable than that of their competitor across the river. The Bradfords had not even begun construction on their railroad. Until they finished it, they were sure to lose most, if not all, of their customers to Ruckel and Olmstead.

Daniel was exactly where Ainsworth and Thompson wanted him. His vulnerable position presented what Ainsworth later described, using his favorite war metaphor, the perfect timing for him and Thompson to "open our batteries" of persuasion and attempt to convince Daniel to sell his portage.

In May, Ainsworth and Thompson invited Daniel to attend a "Special Board Meeting" at OSN headquarters. They shared with Daniel that they understood and appreciated the precarious situation of his business at the Cascades and the dim outlook of its future, given that Ruckel and Olmstead's railroad would be operational in just a few months. They argued that Daniel's continued investment in his railroad presented significant financial risks, not only because of the high cost of the project but also because, once the railroad was completed, Ruckel and Olmstead would likely continue their attacks on Bradford and Company by undercutting their rates and upgrading their facilities. Ainsworth and Thompson proposed a fast, efficient and profitable solution to Daniel's predicament: sell his portage assets and railroad charter to the OSN for cash.

Daniel flatly refused. He was reluctant to forfeit his subsidy contract with the OSN; a lump-sum payment now, Daniel maintained, was not as valuable as three more years of steady monthly income. After hours of heated discussion, Ainsworth, Thompson and Daniel agreed to break and reconvene in two days.

After a second meeting and more arguments, Daniel finally agreed to sell his tramway and railroad charter to the OSN for $20,000 in cash, with the condition that his subsidy contract remain intact. Though it was not their first choice, honoring Daniel's contract with the OSN was just as well for Ainsworth and Thompson, because it allowed them to convince Daniel to accept a lower offer for his portage assets. To convince Daniel to lower his price, Ainsworth and Thompson assured Daniel that he would collect much more money in subsidies over the next three years than he could ever dream of making from the sale of his portage. Daniel was pacified with the prospect and fixated on his future income. Meanwhile, Ainsworth and

When the OSN encountered financial problems, Ainsworth turned to San Francisco banker William Ralston for loans. They met at Ralston's country estate, shown here. *Courtesy of Library of Congress.*

Upper Cascades, Washington Territory, 1867. The OSN wharf and portage railroad terminus are at right. *Courtesy of Oregon Historical Society.*

Thompson congratulated themselves on reaching the first major milestone in their scheme.

After the sale closed, the board immediately authorized construction of a narrow-gauge railroad over Daniel's six miles of right-of-way at the Cascades. Work on the OSN's railroad from The Dalles to Celilo was abruptly halted, and the construction gang, machinery and material were transferred to the Upper Cascades. After the crews started grading on the Washington riverbank, the board dispatched Ainsworth to San Francisco to purchase tracks and obtain a loan to fund construction. In a stroke of luck—Ainsworth called it "providence"—he found a single lot of twenty miles of track, the exact amount needed for both OSN railroads. The track and a loan of $50,000 were acquired on easy terms from banker William Ralston, an old friend of both Ainsworth and Jacob Kamm from their Mississippi River days.

TAKING THE OREGON SHORE

When Ruckel and Olmstead witnessed the two-hundred-man crew at work across the river, they were furious. Still refusing to attend any OSN board meetings, they were unaware of Daniel's sale of his portage and the board's decision to transfer construction from The Dalles to the Cascades. Ruckel and Olmstead had assumed they had delivered the final blow to Bradford and Company, whose tramway had lain idle for months while the Oregon portage enjoyed all the business. Now, Ruckel and Olmstead were once again faced with impending defeat as a longer railroad, built of stronger material to support larger locomotives and passenger and freight cars, would be installed and operational in a matter of months. They expressed their outrage by mailing written threats to Ainsworth.

The tables had abruptly turned against Ruckel and Olmstead, presenting the opportunity for Ainsworth and Thompson to make their next move in executing their secret plan. They repeated the same process they had employed on Daniel, meeting with Ruckel and Olmstead without any other board members present, painting a precarious picture of their portage's future and offering to buy their assets to save them from what they framed as impending financial ruin. Like Daniel, Ruckel and Olmstead refused and remained reluctant to forfeit their subsidy contract with the OSN.

In October, after seasonal traffic over their portage had slacked considerably and their incomes were dramatically reduced, Ruckel and Olmstead were forced to admit that Ainsworth and Thompson may have been correct in their grim prediction of the fate of the Oregon portage. Panicked because he and Ruckel were falling short of covering the large monthly interest payments due on their mounting debt, Olmstead urgently wrote to Ainsworth that he was interested in resuming negotiations to sell the portage to the OSN.

Ainsworth met with Ruckel and Olmstead to discuss terms and then returned to the board to present their proposed price of $175,000. Now that the leverage had shifted to the OSN, the board took advantage of the new conditions, refused Ruckel and Olmstead's price and neglected to submit a counteroffer. The next day, Ainsworth met with Ruckel and Olmstead to present the board's response and negotiate a lower price. After a full day of exhausting debate, Ruckel and Olmstead finally agreed to accept $155,000 with financing, provided $115,000 was paid up front. That evening, the OSN Board of Directors accepted the offer.

A key provision of the OSN's purchase agreement with Ruckel and Olmstead was verbal and not recorded in the bill of sale or board meeting minutes for the transaction. It was the final and most controversial step of Ainsworth and Thompson's plan and what Ainsworth was referring to when he wrote in his memoirs that he manipulated the portage owners "as a cat's paw" against each other.

During his private negotiations with Ruckel and Olmstead, Ainsworth agreed to recommend that the OSN Board of Directors approve purchasing the Oregon portage on one condition: that Ruckel and Olmstead not only forfeit their right to subsidies per their contract with the OSN but also terminate the contract for all parties, including Bradford and Company. To help protect himself and the board from Daniel's retribution, Ainsworth convinced Olmstead to perform the unpleasant task of notifying Daniel that the contract was, as of the date of the sale of the Oregon portage, void, absolving the OSN from making three years of monthly payments.

It took a full year, but by the end of 1862, Ainsworth and Thompson's plan to take over the portages was complete. The OSN's entire transportation system, both overland and on the water, was now owned by the company. With full control at the Cascades, the OSN could now improve facilities to better accommodate demand and effectively reduce future risk of expensive damage claims.

Though in his memoirs Ainsworth admitted that his and Thompson's scheme to break the OSN's subsidy contract with the Cascades portage owners "was not the style of doing business that was agreeable to me," he rationalized that they had no other choice. "We had to work as best we could with the material in hand," Ainsworth explained to his family of the affair. In all, Ainsworth looked back on the secret plan to acquire the Cascades portages as one of the most important management achievements in the OSN's history, one that "The O.S.N. Co.," Ainsworth proudly proclaimed, "must ever be indebted to Thompson and myself."

7

THE ENEMY ONSLAUGHT

I n 1862, the horrors of the battles of Shiloh, Harpers Ferry and Fredericksburg forced the eastern states to let go of their naive prediction that the Union-Confederate dispute would result in a brief conflict with a few skirmishes and instead mobilize for a long, resource-draining and destructive war.

On the opposite side of the continent, thousands of miles from the bloody front lines, the Pacific Northwest remained distracted from eastern troubles with its continued pursuit of gold.

The OSN Board of Directors' prediction proved accurate: there was another rush to the Nez Perce reservation in 1862, where more gold deposits were discovered on the Salmon and Powder Rivers. As early as February, prospectors, mostly from California, overwhelmed the Columbia River and its shoreside communities. Portland's streets were crammed with wagons, and its boardinghouses rarely contained vacancies throughout most of the year. In May, Wells Fargo newspaper deliveries to The Dalles and Portland circulated a rumor that as much as $500,000 in gold was being pulled out of the Salmon per day. With record demand for digging rights, trading fractional ownership in mining claims became a new and lucrative speculation strategy.

The OSN's business in 1862 was in many ways a repeat of the year before, except with an even larger volume. The seasonal increase in traffic up the Columbia River again taxed the OSN's transportation system beyond its capacity. Every steamboat and sailing vessel owned and charted by the company was kept in constant motion during daylight hours. It was still not enough to meet demand; freight piled up again at the portages, and the OSN was forced to turn away clamoring customers at its wharf in Portland. By the end of 1862, the manifests revealed that the company had shipped over twice the amount of tonnage than that shipped during the previous year.

Ironically, though revenue was much higher, the OSN suffered financially in 1862. A historic flooding event that forced residents of The Dalles into the hills caused extensive damage to company property and required expensive repairs. But the heaviest expenditures for the year were for the purchases of the portages and the first phases of railroad construction. The costs associated with these projects—totaling at least $250,000 in 1862 alone—were covered by the company's profits and outside loans. The board implemented strategies to offset other costs, such as discontinuing dividend payments.

Still, the board maintained its confidence in the OSN's future. It kept its gaze fixated on long-term goals: reincorporating in Oregon, doubling its capital stock to $2 million and extending the scope of its services to include steam navigation on the Columbia River up to the forty-ninth parallel, Fort Boise on the Snake, Eugene City on the Willamette and on "all oceans." After reincorporating, the OSN Board of Directors packed up its headquarters in Vancouver and moved to its new office at the corner of Front and Ash Streets in Portland, a short walk from the OSN's wharf.

THE CHALLENGERS

After two years of dominating regional transportation and establishing itself as a seemingly permanent fixture in the economic and physical landscapes of the Columbia and Willamette valleys, the OSN came into the public's field of vision and, consequently, wove itself into the social fabric of the region. The nature of a community's transactions with the OSN largely determined that community's attitudes about the company.

To Lewiston, the OSN was its savior. Because of the steady flow of miners and dry goods the company deposited at the town's waterfront, the OSN helped it grow and inadvertently regulated its commodity markets. In Portland, the OSN became a home-grown hero of which its business community was staunchly proud. Specifically, the city admired the company's untouchable status and wealth. Portland's *Morning Oregonian* newspaper became an early and loyal OSN supporter. "With the superior advantages they possess, together with an immense capital," the newspaper boasted of the OSN in 1862, "it is but reasonable to suppose that no other company can hope to successfully compete with them." The *Oregonian* went as far as to warn would-be competitors not to threaten its favorite steamboat company's status: "It is folly to undertake to run in opposition to such a powerful company."

Upper Columbia communities did not share Portland's enthusiasm for the OSN. These remote shoreside settlements, hundreds of miles from company headquarters, interacted with the OSN sparingly, usually when steamboats came and left in a hurry. The population in this part of the Pacific Northwest, dominated by farmers often low on cash, suffered most at the mercy of the OSN's high rates.

No upper Columbia community was as loud or persistent a protestor against the OSN as The Dalles. When word spread through town that the company planned to build a railroad to Celilo, skeptical newspaper editors dismissed the plan as a "ruse." When the OSN abruptly shut down construction and transferred the operation to the Cascades, the distrust of The Dalles citizens was affirmed, and local newspaper editors expressed their inflamed indignation about the company and its leadership. Ainsworth's refusal to be interviewed by journalists only bolstered the Jacksonian narrative adopted by upper river settlers that the OSN embodied everything that farmers hated about capitalism. They viewed the company as an aristocratic, unfeeling and unscrupulous institution obsessed with chasing profits at the expense of the Northwest's humble yeomanry.

The OSN's success, the overwhelming demand for river transportation and the calls for better service at The Dalles presented an opportunity for enterprising individuals, undeterred by risk, who possessed enough capital to get into the steamboat business. In 1862, two such individuals, sea captain Alexander Ankeny and merchant Henry Corbett, recognized this opportunity, quickly incorporated the Merchants Transportation Line (MTL) and invested in the construction of three small steamboats: one for service from Portland to the Cascades, another from the Cascades to The Dalles and a third from Celilo to Lewiston. The MTL's steamers were launched and ready to compete with the OSN's line by August, still enough time to profit from the high-traffic season.

Portland, Oregon, looking northeast, late 1860s. *Courtesy of Oregon Historical Society.*

Cattle farming in eastern Oregon. Ranchers preferred shipping their livestock on the OSN's steamboats over driving them across the Cascade Mountains. *Courtesy of Oregon Historical Society.*

Left: To wilderness homesteaders like these near Cape Horn, Washington Territory, the OSN's steamboats were their primary connection with the outside world. *Courtesy of Oregon Historical Society.*

Right: Like most Portland merchant-politicians, Henry Corbett dabbled in transportation. Once a competitor of the OSN, Corbett eventually joined its board. *Courtesy of Oregon Historical Society.*

NEW COMPETITORS

Ainsworth was intensely fearful of the threat of competition. He coped with this fear by adopting highly aggressive, even ruthless, policies to not just overcome but also eliminate competition quickly and efficiently. "When we made a fight, we took them in as prisoners," Ainsworth once described the OSN's approach to dealing with competition. "They came in and we got hold of the locks....It [was] always our policy that somebody had to be killed." Jacob Kamm, Ainsworth's oldest friend on the OSN Board of Directors, once wrote that his partner "would not tolerate serious competition, and went for [his] rivals with vigor…no quarter was to be given…it must be a fight to a finish."

Frustratingly for Ainsworth, when the MTL launched its steamboats on the Columbia River, the OSN could hardly afford to fight. The company was in the worst financial shape of its nineteen-year history due to the recent expenditures of purchasing the portages and constructing two railroads. Ainsworth was gravely concerned that the OSN's situation would be made even worse if it were forced to fight an expensive rate war.

Eventually, Ainsworth realized that a fight was inevitable. As the MTL's new steamboat at The Dalles prepared to depart for its maiden voyage downriver, a desperate Ainsworth made sure the OSN was ready to fire the first shot of the rate war. He instructed his local agent to station himself at The Dalles waterfront and, using whatever means necessary, ensure that the MTL's vessel "got no passengers whatever" and convince them to instead board the OSN's steamer "at some price that would get them all, if only a dollar a head." At Portland headquarters, a highly anxious Ainsworth told Kamm that he planned to check the passenger list when the OSN steamboat bearing the MTL passengers arrived in Portland. If a single MTL passenger was missing, Ainsworth planned to reprimand the OSN's agent at The Dalles.

Meanwhile, Ainsworth busied himself attempting to persuade Ankeny and Corbett to sell. They initially balked, but after six months of losing money during their competition with the OSN, the MTL finally agreed to cut its losses and sell. The OSN could ill afford the $50,000 it paid to purchase the MTL's fleet, but Ainsworth was relieved to have been able to eliminate a competitor, end the expensive rate war and restore the OSN's rates to its usual high levels.

THE PEOPLE'S WAR

Just one month after the OSN eliminated its first competitor, another adversary emerged to threaten the financially weak company. Unlike the MTL's small partnership of two, this newest Columbia River steamboat company benefited from the support of a large network of investors, mostly from communities that opposed the OSN, such as The Dalles. The new company was incorporated by and for farmers in the late 1850s and named itself the People's Transportation Company (PTC) to reflect its populist agenda. The PTC opened its business with a fleet of small and economically built steamboats to service the many remote landings of the Willamette River, where farmers from distant sections of the valley traveled to deposit their harvests for shipment to the Portland market.

After the OSN was incorporated, PTC management remained attentive to the increasing complaints about high shipping rates on the Columbia River and, at the end of 1862, made a move to compete with the OSN. Journalists at the normally loyal *Morning Oregonian* heard and passed along to their readers the rumor that the PTC was planning on building "several fine steamers," which were expected to be "superior to those of the Oregon Steam Navigation Company in every respect." The *Oregonian* added an applause of what it interpreted as the PTC's advancement of free trade in Oregon, predicting that the new service on the Columbia River "will thus preserve the just rights and privileges of every individual and...the interests and advancement of poorer classes."

The PTC launched three steamboats in the spring of 1863. Unlike the MTL, the PTC spared no expense when constructing its Columbia River fleet; each vessel was comparable to the OSN's steamboats in size, speed and cabin comfort. The PTC's stern-wheeler *E.D. Baker*, built for service from Portland to the Cascades, proved much faster than the OSN's decade-old side-wheeler *Wilson G. Hunt*, a fact that PTC captains reminded the *Hunt*'s crews and passengers whenever the two steamboats challenged each other to a race. Above the Cascades, the appearance of the PTC's luxurious side-wheeler *Iris* made the OSN's *Hassalo* and *Idaho* look small, underpowered and outdated. Passengers flocked to the PTC for the fastest, newest and most comfortable travel on the Columbia, and shippers took advantage of discounted rates.

The OSN lost a large amount of business to the PTC in a matter of weeks. Ainsworth had no choice but to initiate another rate war by undercutting the PTC's rates. The PTC fired back by further undercutting

The OSN purchased the *Wilson G. Hunt* from Puget Sound owners for service on the Columbia River during the gold rush. *Courtesy of Multnomah County Library.*

The *Iris* was built by the People's Transportation Company to compete with the OSN, which quickly purchased her. *Courtesy of Multnomah County Library.*

the OSN, and the rounds continued until the OSN slashed its prices in some cases by more than 90 percent. Agents from both companies began bidding against each other for passengers at steamboat landings along the Columbia.

On the lower river, customers patronized whichever company charged the lowest rates. But on the upper Columbia, where farmers dominated the freight market, the PTC drew a loyal following of patrons who were willing to purchase their tickets at any price. These passionate PTC supporters once triggered a standoff between the OSN and shippers and passengers above The Dalles when, at Lewiston, the OSN offered a crowd of 135 PTC customers passage to Portland free of charge. Only 10 of the group took the offer; the rest boarded the PTC steamboat and paid five dollars per ticket.

Ainsworth panicked. After just one month of competition with the PTC, the rate war had pummeled the OSN into a state of financial emergency. A desperate Ainsworth called an impromptu board meeting to develop a crisis response plan, tasking the team with determining how to reduce as many expenses as possible, as fast as possible. The board decided to first issue salary cuts, Ainsworth himself forfeiting nearly half of his pay. The board also launched initiatives to raise cash by dispatching Ainsworth to San Francisco to visit his old friend William Ralston and apply for another loan. The board also made plans to sell off some of the OSN's real estate portfolio.

In addition to the damage already done to the OSN's balance sheet over the previous year due to the company's borrowing of hundreds of thousands of dollars in loans, spending tens of thousands on the construction of new steamboats and a recent sudden decrease in revenue, the near future looked even more expensive for the OSN. The continued rate war with the PTC ensured continued revenue losses, and the total cost of construction of the company's two railroads was approaching $1 million. Ainsworth, the OSN Board of Directors and the rest of the OSN's stockholders had ample reason to believe that the days of the large company's monopoly, profitability and possibly very existence were over.

8

VICTORY

L uckily for the OSN and its shareholders, the PTC also began to buckle under the weight of mounting financial stress. Building beautiful steamboats was expensive and operating them at thin profit margins or losses proved even more costly. One month after the OSN began making cuts, the PTC exhausted all its available capital and began a deep dive into debt.

By the third month of their competition, both the PTC and OSN were eager to end their rate war. William Ladd, who was then banker for both the OSN and the PTC, brokered a deal with PTC owners that secured each company's future financial success: the OSN purchased the PTC's Columbia River steamboat fleet and sold the PTC all three of its steamboats operating on the Willamette. The transaction restored the OSN's monopoly on the Columbia and gave the PTC a monopoly over the Willamette. To discourage the former rival from competing against the OSN in the future, Ainsworth agreed to pay the cash-strapped PTC a yearly subsidy of $10,000 if it promised to never again enter the Columbia. The deal was made just in time for the PTC, whose managers were forced to face the reality that the OSN, with its superior ability to generate and secure more capital, would inevitably pull ahead in their competition and establish an unchallengeable lead.

In addition to its access to money, the OSN owned far more valuable fixed assets than the PTC. The OSN's two railroads were complete by April,

Left: OSN rail yard at Lower Cascades. From left to right: turntable, locomotive shed and car shed. *Courtesy of Oregon Historical Society.*

Below: The OSN's fleet on The Dalles–Cascades route, late 1860s. From left to right: *Dalles, Idaho* and *Iris. Courtesy of Oregon Historical Society.*

rolling stock was delivered and installed in May and regular rail service between the Upper and Lower Cascades and between The Dalles and Celilo steamboat landings was inaugurated in June. Though the PTC once claimed the newest and most stately steamboats on the Columbia, the OSN, soon after purchasing the PTC fleet, launched two new and powerful stern-wheelers above Celilo and the handsomest example of marine engineering yet seen above the Cascades: a 150-foot-long floating palace of a side-wheeler christened the *Oneonta*.

After ending their rate war with the PTC, the OSN's financial future looked much brighter. Rates were restored to their previously high levels—tripling the cost of steamboat passage on the Columbia River from when the PTC was in operation—and the board secured three

Top: OSN railroad terminus at The Dalles. At right are the car shed, roundtable, locomotive shed and ticket office. *Courtesy of Oregon Historical Society.*

Bottom: The side-wheeler *Oneonta* at Upper Cascades steamboat landing. She was the pride of the OSN fleet when this photo was taken in 1867. *Courtesy of Oregon Historical Society.*

government contracts: two to ship the U.S. Mail from Portland to Walla Walla for a yearly subsidy of $24,000 and another to ship military supplies from Fort Vancouver to Wallula at a rate of $20 per ton.

BIGGER, BETTER, RICHER

After eliminating its most significant threat, the OSN entered a phase of uninterrupted prosperity. Throughout the rest of 1863 and in 1864, the OSN added a total of nine steamboats to its fleet, some of which were larger and more luxuriously designed and furnished than any steamboat that had previously plied Pacific Northwest waters. Most impressive was the side-wheeler *New World*, which the OSN purchased to service its route from Portland to the Cascades. At 275 feet long, the *New World* dwarfed every other watercraft on the Columbia and Willamette Rivers and, with its thirty-five plush staterooms, provided passengers a level of extravagance previously unknown to travelers north of San Francisco.

The OSN Board of Directors also invested in new facilities at the company's steamboat landings. They purchased a hotel and floating wharf at Wallula and built another at The Dalles. The board drew up plans to construct the second-longest wharf on the Portland waterfront and at the Celilo steamboat landing, the longest warehouse on the West Coast. At the termini of the company's two railroads, the OSN constructed passenger and freight depots, turntables, car sheds, machine shops and administrative offices. To optimize communication and logistics coordination between The Dalles and Celilo, the OSN installed and inaugurated the first telegraph service in the Northwest along the company's fifteen-mile railroad.

Portlanders swelled with pride as they watched the OSN's progress. The *Morning Oregonian* publicly praised Ainsworth and the board for their hard work, resolving that they deserved "great credit for the continued and costly improvements by which they make a trip to the mines both comfortable and pleasant."

The OSN's board and shareholders were more pleased about the company's financial results. Despite losing a significant amount of business to the MTL and PTC during the first half of the high traffic season, the OSN managed to produce $1.3 million in revenue by the end of 1863. More surprising, even after borrowing heavily to fund the construction and acquisition of its most expensive fixed assets, the OSN not only paid back all its debt but also produced a net profit of $173,000 for the period December

Above: Morning at the OSN's Celilo steamboat landing and railroad terminus. The warehouse was split into three sections, each to accommodate a different water level. *Courtesy of Oregon Historical Society*.

Left: OSN machine shop and brass foundry at The Dalles. Locomotives and cars were repaired at this facility. *Courtesy of Oregon Historical Society*.

1862 through September 1863. In 1864, the board determined it was in sound enough financial shape to resume dividend payments. There was more reason than ever to believe that the OSN's stress-filled days of painful growth were over, and stability and prosperity lay ahead.

Decreasing the OSN's future risk was the fact that the influence of the former portage owners was weaker than ever. When Daniel Bradford presented a claim to the board to recover the subsidy payments he lost after Ainsworth persuaded Harrison Olmstead to terminate their contract, Ainsworth garnered sufficient voting support to reject the claim. Since selling their businesses to the OSN, the former portage owners had gone their separate ways and used their cash to pursue new speculation schemes and enjoy the leisure of semi-retirement. Both Daniel and Olmstead resigned from the OSN Board of Directors and returned east with their families. Joseph Ruckel remained in Oregon and kept his seat on the board, but his voting power was negligible, and he maintained only a passive interest in the company. His attention was now being divided between his new mining investments east of the Columbia River and fighting a lawsuit in the Portland courts.

With the former portage owners effectively disconnected from the daily affairs of the OSN, Ainsworth and Thompson looked forward to unencumbered progress toward executing their long-term expansion plans for the company. Unbeknownst to Ainsworth and Thompson, the appearance of the former portage owners' inactivity was deceiving; behind closed doors, their influence had grown more powerful than ever.

9

THE COUP

Though their involvement was minimal during OSN Board of Director meetings throughout the second half of 1863 and most of 1864, Ruckel, Olmstead and the Bradford brothers were very active in board matters outside the official meetings. During this time, the former portage owners orchestrated a political movement to overthrow Ainsworth's presidency and take control of the company. After Ainsworth found out later about this coup, he held Ruckel and Daniel responsible, rationalizing that the anxious men had launched the campaign because they were "afraid of my power." Though he had employed the same manipulative tactics to take over their portages, Ainsworth condemned Ruckel and Daniel's actions as "very underhanded."

FESTERING DISCORD

Ironically, it was how Ainsworth handled the purchase of the portages that turned the former portage owners against him. Ruckel and Olmstead were furious that Ainsworth neglected to consult them before the board decided to purchase Daniel's assets, robbing them of their opportunities to contribute to the discussions and voting process.

Ainsworth's broken promise to honor Daniel's subsidy contract with the OSN marked a turning point in their relationship. Daniel, who had previously viewed Ainsworth as a close friend, was stunned with surprise and the pain of betrayal when Ainsworth voted to deny Daniel's claim to recover his payments. "The facts…are to me very mortifying," Daniel wrote to Ainsworth after the board meeting. "I…felt that in counselling with you I was getting advice that I could rely upon." Daniel pleaded with Ainsworth, "I do ask to put you in my position.…If you had not a dollar in the case you would act according to your views of right and wrong."

Fortifying the portage owners' resolve to oust Ainsworth was their fundamental disagreement with his policies, such as his tendency to invest the OSN's available cash in its steamboat fleet. Ainsworth had been dissatisfied with the quality of the company's vessels since its inception and made clear to the board his opinion that "earnings *must* be absorbed for some time to come in creating new and more suitable steamers." But the former portage owners, who had no affection or interest in steamboats beyond their potential as a speculation scheme, viewed the company's fleet as excessive, an asset whose expenses should be minimized so that profits from their revenue could be maximized. Daniel was especially outspoken about this view. He once challenged Thompson about the renovation costs of one of the OSN's best steamboats: "Would not the *Wilson G. Hunt* have done as much work this season as though you have not spent $35,000 on her[?]"

Of all the points of contention for Ruckel, Olmstead and the Bradford brothers, it was Ainsworth's policy regarding stock dividends that was the most significant. Ainsworth's aversion to loans—Daniel described it as "a holy horror of debt"—and expenses unrelated to the company's fixed assets influenced his low prioritization of dividends payments. During the OSN's first four years of business, Ainsworth never proposed the payment of dividends or supported the board's motions to issue such payments. During 1862 and 1863, Ainsworth succeeded in swaying the OSN Board of Directors to defer all dividends. But to Ruckel, Olmstead and the Bradford brothers, who entered into the transportation industry primarily to speculate for profits, dividends were critical; these payments not only constituted a large portion of their incomes but also influenced the value of their OSN shares, which made up the bulk of their personal fortunes. Besides increasing their monthly incomes, the former portage owners, savvy to stock speculation strategies, knew that if the OSN made consistent and generous dividend payments, demand for the company's stock would increase, driving up the market price of their shares. Olmstead viewed Ainsworth's prioritization of fixed assets over dividends as robbery of his retirement income. Olmstead, whose OSN shares possessed a par value of $279,000, vented to another board member in 1866: "If the Company would…attend to their legitimate Bus[iness] the stock would pay 2% &

be *worth par*, But no! They must continually have some project on hand to spend the earnings."

Olmstead, Ruckel and the Bradford brothers discovered that they were not the only OSN board members who resented Ainsworth's dividend policy. Simeon Reed and the Ladd brothers, who were also indifferent about the company's steamboats and more focused on minimizing expenses, consistently lobbied for increased dividend payments. After he relocated to New York, John Ladd maintained a close relationship with business partner Reed, and the two corresponded often about how the OSN might be managed, as John put it, "to the advantage of the Stockholders." Like the former portage owners, John was disconnected from the daily business of the company but held on to his shares primarily as a speculation scheme. "The stock suits me," John once flippantly wrote to Reed about his OSN shares, "so long as it pays dividends sufficient to keep me in spending money."

Though they did not nurse strong negative feelings about Ainsworth like the former portage owners, Reed and the Ladd brothers did not enjoy friendly relations with him. Ainsworth was distant with Reed and the Ladds and wary of their agendas, since they were granted stock not because they contributed hard assets to the company but because they owned the debt of the portage businesses. Ainsworth was least impressed with Reed, whom he suspected devoted most of his time and energy to his investments with the Ladds and "gave no thought" to the OSN outside of its board meetings. An annoyed Ainsworth looked on as precious time at the beginning of each meeting was spent briefing Reed on the OSN's developments since the previous meeting, an exercise that Ainsworth was resigned to repeat as much as necessary, lest Reed fail to "vote intelligently" when the board made its policy decisions.

THE TAKEOVER

Ruckel, Olmstead, Reed, the Bradfords and the Ladds were drawn to one another in 1864 and bonded over their disagreement with Ainsworth's policies. They formed a faction and held secret meetings outside of the OSN offices to discuss their feelings, ideas and plans to support one another in advancing their agenda of minimizing expenses, maximizing profits and, above all, increasing dividends.

Even Daniel and Ruckel, once bitter enemies, worked together in achieving their common goals in the coup. In July, the faction devised a plan to resume dividend payments. Daniel and Ruckel called a board meeting and proposed the declaration of a 2 percent dividend. Reed and the Ladd brothers seconded, the faction's majority vote passed to resolution and the payment was immediately issued. The Bradford brothers, still the largest stockholders, received over $7,000.

Next, Daniel persuaded Ruckel and Reed to support his efforts to reverse the board's previous decision to deny his claim for payment of withheld subsidies. At the next official meeting, Daniel proposed to the group that his claim be arbitrated for settlement. When the issue was put to a vote, Ainsworth objected, but Ruckel and Reed joined Daniel's side and their majority carried the motion to resolution.

Then, the faction devised a plan to take advantage of two upcoming vacancies on the OSN Board of Directors. Daniel, flush with dividend cash and content with the promise of much more in the near future, viewed this plan as his opportunity to live out the dream he and his brother had envisioned when they sailed west fourteen years earlier. He made arrangements to cut his ties to Portland, return to his wife and son in Massachusetts and enjoy a retirement of stylish leisure. Daniel would resign from the OSN, leaving vacant his positions of vice-president and director. In order to preserve their control over the company, the faction planned to nominate and elect its members to fill Daniel's previous positions. They chose to nominate Putnam Bradford to fill Daniel's board seat and Reed to take the open position of vice-president, a promotion for both men.

Their plan in place, the faction called another impromptu board meeting, where Daniel presented his official resignation. After the faction accepted, they moved immediately to conduct an election to fill Daniel's positions. Though Ainsworth voted against the faction, his influence was easily overpowered and Putnam and Reed were elected.

The faction deployed their most aggressive scheme at the annual election of company officers in November: to prevent Ainsworth's reelection and install Ruckel as OSN president. Thompson and Jacob Kamm, Ainsworth's most loyal supporters, could not supply enough votes to overcome the faction when it nominated Ruckel, who was quickly elected.

The new faction now occupied the most important executive positions in the OSN, while Ainsworth was demoted to a common minority stockholder. The former portage owners and their supporters finally wielded the power they had long yearned for: effective control of OSN policy, expenses and, most important to them, dividend payments.

Ainsworth, Thompson and Kamm were flabbergasted; they never thought they would live to see the day that Joseph Ruckel, who had a well-known history of demonstrating poor management skills and making poorer financial decisions, would command the OSN. Ainsworth packed up his effects at company headquarters and retired to his mansion uptown to refocus his attention on his mining and real estate investments. Thompson was so distraught that he considered cutting all ties with the OSN and moving back to California. Kamm refused to work for Ruckel and resigned from the board.

Though Ruckel won the election, the war for power over the OSN was not over for Ainsworth and Thompson. Their outrage and discouragement were not enough to convince them to give up their dreams for the company's future.

10

RECLAIMING THE THRONE

John Ladd was ecstatic when he received a telegram with news of Ruckel's victory. Now that his trusty business partner, Reed, was vice-president and in control of the company's finances, John found a new confidence in the OSN's future. "Make no doubt but every thing will go along smoothly," John congratulated Reed, "you are better able and competent to look after the interests of the Co than those who have had the management thus far." In response to Reed's report of the negative reactions displayed by Ainsworth, Thompson and Kamm, Ladd was unfazed, reassuring Reed that they would "get over their fret after a while."

Daniel was also pleased. He believed that the OSN stockholders living on the East Coast, ignorant of daily operations and emotionally detached from assets, possessed superior managerial judgment compared to Portland board members. Daniel rationalized—ironically, given his history of displaying volatile behavior during meetings—that local managers were subject to what he described as "jealousies & heartburnings," which influenced them to make emotionally distorted decisions about policies and ultimately put the OSN at risk.

Once in power, the Ruckel faction wasted no time in asserting their agenda. Less than one month after the election, the new OSN leadership declared a 4 percent dividend, one of the highest such payments issued in the company's history. The faction next moved forward with arbitrating Daniel's claim and settled it, writing him a check for $22,000. Meanwhile, Reed launched a campaign to reduce the OSN's overhead expenses, starting with the implementation of wage reductions for most employees, whom he judged were overpaid or, as Reed put it, had "had their *own way* for a long time."

Reed poured himself into his work on the OSN's finances and quickly became overwhelmed. A few months into his new role, it became painfully obvious to Reed that Ainsworth, Thompson and Kamm had been correct in suspecting that Ruckel did not possess the management skills, temperament or knowledge of the OSN necessary to effectively fulfill his duties as president. Ruckel quickly piled responsibilities on Reed and soon relied on him to make daily operational decisions. After having spent his first four years on the board as a passive meeting attendee, Reed realized there was much he needed to learn about the OSN in order to not only effectively perform his new job as vice-president but also prevent Ruckel from negatively impacting the company's future with his poor management decisions.

A desperate Reed abandoned his loyalty to the Ruckel faction and sought advice from the stockholder who knew the most about the OSN: John Ainsworth. Reed began to meet in secret with Ainsworth and Thompson to debrief board meeting proceedings, discuss recent developments in the business and explore ideas for future growth. Eventually, Ainsworth, in effect, began controlling the OSN through Reed, mentoring and advising him on both daily operational decisions and long-term planning.

During their private sessions, Ainsworth and Thompson educated Reed on the history of the former portage owners and the years of financial and emotional stress caused by their self-serving and difficult behavior. In learning these details, Reed realized that he had made a grave mistake in trusting the former portage owners and supporting them in their faction.

The Counterattack

An enlightened Reed shared his new insights and feelings about the former portage owners with the Ladd brothers. William responded by immediately defecting from the faction and joining Reed in his new convictions. John was surprised but supportive when he learned of Reed's and William's new loyalties; he remained deferential to their judgment regarding OSN affairs because of their regular attendance at board meetings. Unlike Daniel, John believed William and Reed accessed more valuable, accurate and timely information than he could ever expect three thousand miles away in New York. "You and William are on the spot," John wrote in response to Reed's revelation, "know all the 'ins and outs'…and of course see through the true state of circumstances." Besides, John finally admitted, he had never trusted Daniel, whom he came to realize possessed neither a work ethic nor scruples. Confidentially to Reed, John observed that Daniel "rather likes to sit quietly down, have others do the work and he reap the reward."

Reed also shared with the Ladds that through his lengthy discussions with Ainsworth and Thompson about the OSN's future, he had come to appreciate their expansionist agenda. Having each heard reports of recent incorporations of stagecoach companies and new steamboat operators east of the Columbia River, Ainsworth, Thompson and Reed agreed that the OSN must move aggressively before competition stole their chance to profit from the latest fleeting rush to the new mines in the Idaho Territory.

There was also the matter of the Northern Pacific Railway (NPR), which was incorporated during the summer of 1864 to construct the first transcontinental railroad to the Pacific Northwest. Planning for the railroad was still in its early stages, and Ainsworth, Reed and Thompson perceived an opportunity to negotiate a deal with the larger and much more capital-intensive NPR to connect the OSN's line with its railroad or even merge the two companies.

Executing the vision for the OSN's future now shared by Ainsworth, Thompson and Reed would require the exact strategy that the Ruckel faction made it their most urgent priority to abolish: a policy of investing profits into fixed assets and avoiding the expense of dividends payments. Expansion of the OSN's line into the Idaho and Montana markets called for heavy expenditures in steamboat, wharf and warehouse construction. A contract with the NPR could require even more capital to upgrade the OSN's fleet, railroads and their auxiliary facilities. Though he formerly agreed with the Ruckel faction's objections to spending on such projects— especially if it negatively impacted dividends—Reed had completed a full conversion to Ainsworth's philosophy that such expenditures were, Reed now claimed, "not a matter of choice, but necessity."

John Ladd, like his brother William, came to agree with Reed, Ainsworth and Thompson in regard to their expansion agenda, and a new faction was formed. To most of the OSN Board of Directors and stockholders, Ainsworth and Thompson were now outsiders stripped of their power, but uptown at Ainsworth's and Thompson's mansions, the six men entered what Ainsworth referred to in his diary as a "private agreement" to advance their expansion policies at the OSN. Like the Ruckel regime, the new faction would rely on the combined power of their votes during board meetings to gain majority approval of such policies as new fixed asset construction and purchases, dividend decreases and engagement with the NPR. Ainsworth felt so optimistic about the potential of the new faction's "agreement" that before their plan was implemented, he purchased as much OSN stock as he could afford.

The success of the new faction's plan hinged on a policy of strict secrecy. All communication about the plan would remain confidential— easily achieved, it seemed, since most of the group could meet outside the OSN's board meetings and therefore avoid the interception of letters and telegrams. In the group's correspondence with John in New York, each letter containing sensitive information would be marked "confidential." All other letters would be marked "official," and in these communications, the new faction agreed that their secret plans were "not to be alluded to" and the writer would include information "only of such matters as can be Shown to Dan[iel]" and other outsiders.

To discourage expense-averse stockholders from voting against the expansion campaigns proposed by the new faction, they began to conceal documents containing information related to the company's expenses. Reed, who controlled expense and all other pertinent financial data at the OSN, rationalized the principle of the new practice to John, claiming that it was "in-advisable for the stockholders to know the result of the years business… and…funds on hand." It was one thing for board members to remain privy to the OSN's financial condition, but as far as other stockholders, Reed believed, the less they knew about the OSN's finances, the better. "There are many things," Reed claimed, "connected with the prudent management of the Company's business, which it would be inexpedient for the stockholders… to be apprised of."

Despite their efforts to maintain secrecy, word about Reed's new alliance with Ainsworth leaked and reached Daniel in Massachusetts. Daniel was furious when he heard that a new faction had been formed without his knowledge and that his nemesis, Ainsworth, was its leader. Having cultivated what he thought was a close relationship with Reed over their shared critical views of Ainsworth's policies, Daniel felt betrayed, much as he had with Ainsworth a few years earlier. "In the position I occupy toward the Company," Daniel scolded Reed in a letter, "am I not entitled to as much or more confidence than Capt. Ainsworth[?] 'tis very annoying.…I have to get news of importance in the Companies affairs from *Outsiders*…so much for your [damned] Secrets."

THE TAKEOVER

Whether or not he became aware of the new faction's plans is not known, but in August 1865, Ruckel abruptly resigned and left Portland forever. In Ainsworth's view, it was Ruckel's "utter unfitness for the position" that "forced" him to resign.

Ruckel's departure was the best stroke of fortune that could have occurred for the new faction. The most significant obstacle in executing their plan was removed, and the group could begin implementing their initiatives. The day the board accepted Ruckel's resignation, in keeping with the OSN's constitution, Reed was automatically promoted to fill the open presidency. Thompson was then elected to take Reed's former position as vice-president.

The new faction was now the new regime. The group immediately went to work instituting policy changes to implement their expansion agenda. At the first board meeting following Ruckel's resignation, Reed, Thompson and William Ladd supplied the necessary votes to approve the construction of a new steamboat on the Snake River, the purchase of a wharf in Portland and the reduction of dividends to a paltry .5 percent, the lowest yet paid in the OSN's five-year history.

Next, the new regime addressed one of their highest priorities: withholding the OSN's financial information from anyone outside their group. To this end, they staged what was meant to appear to be a routine policy change. When Reed opened the next annual stockholder meeting with the usual motioning to read the company's year-end financial report, Thompson interrupted with another motion, to vote that the practice of reading the report "be dispensed with." Thompson and William quickly supplied enough votes to carry the motion, Reed ordered the report filed in an undisclosed location and the meeting proceeded to other business.

The new faction's takeover of the OSN was complete when, at the company's annual election of company officers in November, Ainsworth was reelected as president and Reed as vice-president. Conveniently, only Ainsworth, Reed, Thompson, William and the company secretary were present for voting.

11

CHALLENGE AFTER CHALLENGE

As the U.S. government began to implement its Reconstruction program to assist the country's recovery from the Civil War, the OSN's new regime implemented its own program to reconstruct the company to support large-scale and long-term expansion.

Early in 1866, just a few months after reclaiming the presidency, Ainsworth took bold steps to prepare the OSN for the next Pacific Northwest gold rush, which this year was to Montana's Blackfoot Mountains. He obtained approval to use company capital to subsidize the construction of a stagecoach road to connect the Columbia River to Montana and engaged in "long talks" with the OSN's former critics, business owners at The Dalles, to incorporate a subsidiary company for the purpose of inaugurating the first steamboat service in Montana. By March, the OSN was operating its newest steamboat on the Snake River from Olds Ferry to Boise City, adding to the company's fleet of at least ten steamers shuttling passengers and freight between Astoria and Lewiston. The *Morning Oregonian* sang praises of the OSN's opening of eight hundred miles of safe river navigation.

Meanwhile, the new regime took its first major steps toward engaging with one of the recently incorporated transcontinental railroads. The OSN Board of Directors agreed to send Reed to Washington, D.C., where, leveraging his connections in Congress—and Congress's connections with railroad executives—he would lobby for a direct connection between the OSN and either the Union Pacific, Central Pacific or Northern Pacific.

Executing the new regime's expansion agenda brought Ainsworth, Thompson and Reed closer than ever. Their private meetings outside the OSN offices continued; they not only strategized about company policy but also traded securities and real estate, invested in mining companies together and borrowed money from one another and the OSN. They began to share their leisure time, strolling the streets of downtown Portland side by side. They were seen together in public so much that Portland citizens began to refer to the three men as the "triumvirate." It was a moniker of which Ainsworth was immensely proud.

THE IMPOSSIBLE STEAMSHIP

Taking up much of the new regime's available time and other resources was a controversial project inherited from the Ruckel regime. Shortly after Ruckel took office, he and his supporters determined to break into the coastal shipping trade by approving the construction of the largest steamship ever owned by the OSN. The Ruckel regime perceived an opportunity to profit from challenging the Pacific Mail Steamship Company's monopoly of the passenger trade between San Francisco and Portland, improving service for Pacific Northwest merchants and, most important to Reed, reclaiming traffic from the new stagecoach lines out of Northern California, which were fast encroaching on the OSN's new river service to the new Boise mining camps. Ainsworth, ever a proponent for expanding the OSN's fleet, was forced to admit that he appreciated the project. Because of their proximity to New York shipyards, Daniel and John Ladd were assigned charge of the steamship's construction.

Daniel's new assignment suited him well. Bored of the slow pace of his retirement in rural Massachusetts—and his prescribed abstinence from alcohol—Daniel was eager to embark on a new adventure. He left his family and moved into the Metropolitan Hotel, one of New York's most glamorous hostelries. Between business meetings with John, Daniel indulged in the fashionable recreational habits of the New England elite: dressing in flashy clothing, eating at expensive restaurants, passing weekends at the Saratoga Springs resort, attending horse races and socializing with prominent citizens.

Daniel's new lifestyle lifted his spirits. He wrote to Reed often to report on the celebrities he met, such as former Union army generals. John noticed a marked improvement in Daniel's attitude about the new management of the OSN. "Dan appears Satisfied So far as I can determine," John updated

Reed. "I sincerely hope nothing will come up here after to mar the harmony that Should exist." Despite Daniel's former resentment of Reed and the new regime, John became convinced that Daniel felt "that no more 'bones were to be picked'" with Reed or anyone else on the OSN Board of Directors. Notwithstanding, Daniel warned Reed about his concerns regarding the potential cost of the steamship: "I do not wish to see a dollar spent that is not actually necessary."

Unfortunately for Daniel, the steamship project was plagued with difficulties since its inception and constantly incurred unforeseen costs. The board sought a design for a hull capable of carrying one thousand tons while drawing less than thirteen feet of water, an exceptionally shallow draft for a vessel of such tonnage. John and Daniel concluded after their canvas of New York shipbuilders that such a combination of specifications was impossible. As soon as the board agreed on a new design and work began on the hull, a labor strike at the shipyard halted construction for weeks. This event and the new and expensive design plan quickly drove the bills for the project beyond six figures.

Adding to the project's risks was the potential for a ruinous rate war on the Portland–San Francisco route once the ship was delivered to the West Coast. If more companies put steamships on the route, a rate war was sure to ensue as competition for customers increased. Though the OSN possessed enough capital to weather temporary revenue losses from rate reductions on the Columbia River, ocean shipping was a field with much higher stakes and required operators to withstand much larger losses. The board was aware that the company could not survive the expense of building the steamship, covering its high ongoing operational costs and sustaining deficits. Only the richest steamship owners could afford to survive such rate wars. The OSN board concluded that its best—or only—chance to profit from the project was to be the first to challenge Pacific Mail's monopoly and sell its steamship to a competitor before a rate war began.

In order to help prevent the arousal of interest from competitors, secrecy about the OSN's plan to build the ocean steamship was critical. To this end, the board implemented measures to disguise the project. To prevent telegraph operators from intercepting messages about the steamship and forwarding them to potential competitors, the board created a cipher to disguise content. When construction began on the steamship in New York and the existence of the project became undeniable, John and Daniel posed as decoy owners, reassuring suspicious journalists that they were starting a new company with Portland merchants such as Henry Corbett. Local newspapers such as the *Morning Oregonian* believed the cover-up and reported to their readership accordingly.

The board's fear of competition proved well founded. Shortly after construction on the OSN's steamship began, two competitors invaded the Portland–San Francisco route. The first was "Stagecoach King" Ben Holladay, who quickly incorporated the California, Oregon and Mexico Steamship Company at the end of 1865, purchased two steamships and began challenging Pacific Mail on its route. A few months later, another competitor incorporated, built two steamships and began operating them between Portland and San Francisco. By February 1866, there were no fewer than six steamships on the route and not enough customers to justify high ticket prices. A rate war ensued, and the three lines took turns undercutting one another until their passenger and freight prices were reduced by as much as 50 percent. Under such market conditions, the new regime abandoned its idea of competing in the trade.

But the OSN's large and expensive steamship was almost complete. The new regime determined to finish the project and attempt to wring a profit by making a sale. In the autumn of 1866, the 270-foot long, 42-foot-wide side-wheeler, christened the *Oregonian*, was completed at a total cost of just over $400,000. Though they vowed to never operate her, the new regime believed there was a better market for selling the vessel in California than in New York, and a crew was hired to deliver her to San Francisco. After breaking the record for the fastest passage on the route around South America, Ainsworth became confident he could command a high price for the ship. He secretly instructed John, decoy owner, to personally contact ship owners and offer to sell the *Oregonian* for $450,000. Steamship owner William Webb, who was then establishing a new line from New York to San Francisco, inquired about the offer and entered into negotiations for purchase.

After several months quibbling over the *Oregonian*'s price, the new regime tired of the suspense. "All agree that it is best to accept offer of $350,000," a resigned Ainsworth wrote John. "We are anxious to see the long… and vexatious negotiation closed." Webb paid $300,000 in cash, but the remainder was to be paid by Ben Holladay, who promised Webb $50,000 in exchange for Webb's promise to refrain from competing with Holladay on any of his West Coast steamship routes. When the time came for him to pay, the unscrupulous Holladay hired his attorney to absolve him of the responsibility. The OSN took Holladay to court and won, but it wasn't until five years later that Holladay finally wrote a check to the OSN to cover the remaining $50,000.

Mounting Tensions

The *Oregonian* project was not the only OSN investment that produced a loss in 1866. Spring rains caused flooding that submerged The Dalles railroad, halting operations. Partly as a result of such conditions, construction costs of the company's new Snake River steamboats greatly exceeded their original budgets. When they were launched, the expensive vessels often lay idle for want of fuel, as crews discovered that wood was often scarce in the Idaho interior. Though Reed was doing his best to reduce expenses, as Ainsworth put it, "down to a scratch," the board predicted that by the end of the year, the OSN would barely generate enough revenue to break even on its costs. The new regime agreed that given these circumstances, dividends must be sacrificed. To this effect, payments during 1866 never exceeded 1 percent.

Daniel and Harrison Olmstead disagreed wholeheartedly with the dividend cuts. For them, the decrease in payments could not have come at a worse time. Daniel and Olmstead quickly spent the sizeable payments made during Ruckel's tenure and had become accustomed to their lavish New York lifestyles. Daniel wrote to Reed that Olmstead was building a large country estate in Connecticut, was "living pretty fast" in Manhattan and had complained to Daniel repeatedly that dividends had been too low since Reed gained control of the OSN's finances. Daniel also admitted to Reed that he was strapped for cash and that, although he possessed "unbounded faith in the ultimate results" of the new regime's expansion initiatives, such faith "hardly pays board bills at the Metropolitan Hotel." Daniel reverted to his former blunt tone with Reed and went so far as to allude—or threaten—his and John Ladd's resignation if dividends were not raised: "We have worked for nothing long enough & if we can't pay fair dividends Soon we better Sell out."

Reed attempted to pacify Daniel with reassurances that dividends would soon resume. "I am aware of nothing in the future," Reed wrote in what he marked as an "official" letter to Daniel and John, "that will involve any large expenditure of money.…The way seems clear for paying dividends."

But the payments did not resume. As a result, Daniel became increasingly desperate throughout 1866. He abandoned his pleading with Reed and attempted to establish regular communication with Ainsworth and Thompson, approaching them with some of the best flattery and persuasion he could muster. After receiving a warm enough response from Thompson, Daniel could hardly contain his excitement that he may have sparked the interest of Ainsworth's most trusted ally, a major step in gaining influence over dividend policy. "I am indebted to you," Daniel wrote Thompson in a lengthy and heartfelt letter, "for the Commencement of Correspondence and hope it may lead to the interchange of ideas which may prove of mutual advantage to both as our great interests are so identical our united opinion…should carry great weight." Daniel took advantage of Thompson's attention by attempting to arouse in Thompson a sense of the injustice he saw in Reed's policies. "Have you or I been paid in dividends for the business we put in the hands of the company & Capital invested I say no, and why?" Daniel also tried his best to conjure pity, claiming that dividends had been so low that stockholders like he and Olmstead "had to borrow money to live on."

Like in his correspondence with Reed and Thompson, Daniel mentioned his personal financial difficulties in his letters to Ainsworth and waxed poetic in his emotional appeals to increase payments. "The great future will not be with us," Daniel cried to Ainsworth, "let us feel we have our fill of Glory, and…create a glorious bank account." Daniel reserved large sections of his letters for the purpose of explaining elaborate stock trading schemes and their profit potential if adopted by the OSN Board of Directors. Daniel even proposed to Reed that he apply for a loan to fund higher dividend payments.

Reed was unresponsive to Daniel's concerns. Daniel noticed and grew increasingly frustrated, then vindictive, and attempted to turn Ainsworth against Reed. In his letters to Ainsworth, Daniel spent pages divulging unflattering gossip about Reed. He predicted that Reed's lobbying efforts in Washington, D.C., would prove futile and claimed that Reed presented an air of aloofness when he visited the *Oregonian*'s construction site. Daniel tried pandering to Ainsworth's passion for steamboats to attempt to conjure resentment: "Reed has not bothered himself with the vessel," Daniel claimed, "his taste don't run to Steam Ships." Daniel even went so far as to question Ainsworth's feelings about Reed: "Did I not start in with as good a judgment of human nature as he might have?"

By the end of 1866, Daniel had lost his patience with Reed. He expressed his outrage at the board's new policy of discontinuing its practice of sharing the OSN's financial statements with stockholders. "There is one thing annoys me very much," Daniel confronted Reed, "not one of you who write ever give a figure—How can I form an opinion of the Co and not know what you are doing[?]…This very course of keeping things from me is what keeps me so disgusted with the business." Daniel, who thought he had won Reed over when the two vacationed in New York, once again felt betrayed. "I had hoped you had become somewhat enlightened by your trip East," Daniel shamed Reed. "I *guess* you will fall back into your old ways & views & soon forget you have been here." At the end of one angry letter to Reed, Daniel could no longer contain his emotions and stooped to ridicule: "I am sure I could…make more money out of our Co in one year than you make from four."

The dividend question, which had split the OSN Board of Directors for years, had escalated to a crisis that threatened to rupture the cohesive bond formed among Ainsworth, Thompson and Reed and undermine the power of the company's new regime.

12

TOTAL CONTROL

Fortunately for the OSN, Daniel underestimated Ainsworth's and Thompson's loyalty to Reed and to the vision the three men shared for the OSN's future.

Daniel's attempts to break up the "triumvirate" were not only unsuccessful, but they also served to fuel the resentment Ainsworth and Thompson had long harbored for Daniel. As they discussed his letters in Portland, Ainsworth, Thompson and Reed became increasingly convinced that Daniel would, as he had done since the OSN's incorporation, remain a source of continual stress and conflict for the organization and, most importantly, a major obstacle in the path of the new regime's expansion agenda.

But the crisis that emerged in 1866 over the dividend question did not involve only Daniel. His brother Putnam still attended stockholder meetings in Portland, where he lobbied for Daniel's interests—under Daniel's instruction—and exercised significant voting power as a representative of 19 percent of all outstanding OSN stock. Olmstead also continued to vote, albeit through his attorney in Portland, who attended board meetings.

Unlike Olmstead, the Ladd brothers and the Bradford brothers, most of the stockholders outside of the OSN's board knew little about the company and had been holding on to their shares for years as a passive speculation strategy. This mixed group of men included local politicians, retired merchants, in-laws of board members and investors in Ainsworth's other business ventures. It became clear that the core of the dividend crisis was not just Daniel's individual views and agenda but the fact that fundamental differences existed between the management philosophies of the new regime and other stockholders. To the "triumvirate" and their supporters, all other stockholders presented a serious liability for the OSN's future.

Certainly, if only the new regime controlled every share of OSN stock, their expansion policies could be executed more efficiently. In the fall of 1866, the insiders conspired to do just that, orchestrating yet another elaborate secret plan, this one proving to be one of the most controversial in the company's history.

The New Secret Plan

In order for the new regime to gain control of the OSN's stock, those outside their group needed to be willing to sell their shares. But these outsiders were not disposed to part with them easily; some of the earliest investors had earned a 2,000 percent profit from trading shares and collecting dividends in just six years. Inducing these stalwarts to surrender such a lucrative investment seemed an impossible task.

Instead of attempting to persuade outside stockholders to sell, Ainsworth, Thompson and Reed came up with a secret plan to inspire stockholders to divest their shares of their own volition. As usual, the new regime relied on their control of the company's most pertinent operational and financial information as the most effective tool for carrying out the plan. Again, a strict policy of secrecy became the highest priority to ensure success. As they had practiced during the *Oregonian* project, the new regime exchanged telegrams with one another about the plan in cipher, the keys for which were changed often.

Working in favor of the new regime's secret plan to induce stockholders to sell was the fact that business throughout 1866 had remained unusually slow—an investor's worst fear. In their reports to outside stockholders, Ainsworth, Reed and the Ladd brothers were transparent about record-low traffic volume as operational challenges and the encroachment of competition conspired to threaten the profitability of the entire OSN line. In his reports to Olmstead, John mentioned disappointing revenue results and described a sense of doom about the company's future. "I feel more confident than ever," John wrote Olmstead, "that we will lose [a] great amount of the Columbia River business." John even went so far as to suggest to Olmstead that he was considering selling his OSN shares.

The new regime discussed the recent unfavorable business conditions in a much more optimistic tone among themselves. Mostly, this was because OSN's poor financial performance depressed demand for the company's stock. The decrease in demand lowered the market value of shares, which, although bad for sellers, created a discount for those willing to buy. "Business is very dull indeed," Ainsworth cheerfully wrote in an update to John in New York, "which makes the opportunities to purchase all the better." In the autumn of 1866, Reed excitedly reported to Ainsworth that, based on recent trends in OSN stock sales, he predicted the new regime "shall more than likely pick up…what outside stock we can at 85 cents or less."

As confidence in the OSN's future and stock value declined, the new regime stoked the outside shareholders' anxiety by circulating an alarming and false story about the company. To maximize negative impact, the new regime capitalized on the Portland business community's long-held resentment and fear of their peers in California. They staged a takeover of the OSN by Alvinza Hayward, one of San Francisco's wealthiest mine owners. For the new regime, Hayward was a natural choice, not only because of his reputation as a fearless speculator with seemingly unlimited financial means, but also because they knew and trusted him as a longtime associate in their business ventures outside of the OSN. Ainsworth appealed to Hayward: "Assist us in our programme and we will reciprocate in the right way." Though at first he hesitated, Hayward eventually agreed to participate in the scheme. At the end of 1866, Ainsworth told the Portland press that Hayward planned to purchase enough OSN shares to gain a "controlling interest" in the company. This was true; Hayward did purchase the shares, and there were transaction records produced as proof. However, what was not disclosed to the press was the fact that Hayward planned to purchase the shares not to hold for himself but instead for the new regime, who would buy them back at a later date.

To further increase anxiety and encourage outside stockholders to sell their shares, the new regime staged a panic. Soon after newspapers published stories about Hayward's alleged takeover, Ainsworth informed the press that Jacob Kamm, OSN founder and owner of 10 percent of all outstanding OSN stock, placed an order to sell his entire lot of shares. To anyone outside the new regime's inner circle, the timing of Kamm's sale appeared to indicate that he had lost his confidence in Hayward's alleged takeover. In reality, Ainsworth, Thompson and Reed had made a secret agreement with Kamm to provide capital for starting his own steamboat company on the Puget Sound in exchange for selling his OSN shares at a 20 percent discount.

Panic

The new regime's secret plan proved a success. Anxiety among the outside stockholders grew to a fever pitch. To this group, whose only source of information was hearsay, newspapers and carefully curated reports from Ainsworth, Reed, Thompson and the Ladd brothers, the future of the OSN looked worse than ever. Shortly after the Portland newspapers printed the story about Kamm selling his shares, the outside stockholders panicked and began telegraphing orders to Portland. The Bradford brothers were the first to sell. The board replied that it was "authorized" to purchase the Bradfords' shares at a price 25 percent below their par value. Olmstead followed suit two weeks later, and the board also purchased his shares at a discount. The rest of the outside stockholders sold soon after, and the board enjoyed varying discounts on all their purchases, in some cases by as much as 50 percent.

Covering such a large amount of stock purchases over a period of just a few months required hundreds of thousands of dollars in cash. Instead of using their own personal funds, Ainsworth, Thompson, Reed and the Ladd brothers utilized the OSN's liquid capital—including the proceeds from the sale of the *Oregonian* and current available profits—to pay for the shares. But even with the company's money they were still short. As usual, Ainsworth turned to William Ralston for help in making up the balance. Telegraphing each other in secret code, Ralston quickly agreed to front Ainsworth the funds due to the outside stockholders.

Thanks to Ralston, the new regime was able to complete the goal of their secret plan and gained control of over 96 percent of all outstanding OSN shares. The next annual stockholder meetings felt vastly different from those of previous years. There was more of an air of a casual, fraternal gathering than the business formality of prior meetings, and only the new regime and the company secretary were in attendance. It was a stark contrast to the tension and chaos of the first two years of the OSN's existence, when the hostile portage owners hijacked meetings with their emotional outbursts and threats.

At a board meeting one month later, Ainsworth, Reed, Thompson and William easily went through the motions of re-electing themselves into their same executive positions for next year's term. The four men then made plans to celebrate their victories of not only keeping their former titles but also, more importantly, gaining total control of the OSN. To reward themselves, they motioned, voted and approved the payment of a special dividend of 37 percent, the highest by far that had ever been declared in the company's history. Reed and Thompson were then each granted three months of vacation.

MONTHS LATER, PORTLAND NEWSPAPER reports revealed the truth about Hayward's takeover of the OSN. Many of the company's former outside stockholders, especially Olmstead, were livid and took steps to exact revenge on Ainsworth, Thompson and Reed by filing lawsuits against the OSN to seek compensation for being duped into selling their shares at significant discounts. But Ainsworth and Thompson were far from sympathetic about the plight of the former stockholders. To Ainsworth, the sellers received a fair market price for their shares, considering demand for the company's stock was so low. Even years later, Ainsworth insisted that the new regime "had done nothing but what was perfectly proper, legitimate, legal, and honest in the discharge of our duties."

Both Ainsworth and Thompson desperately wanted to fight the former stockholders in court, but the Ladd brothers felt differently. Concerned about their reputations both in Portland and New York, where their bank opened a new branch, William and John were unwilling to risk being called to testify and the media frenzy that would inevitably follow, should Ainsworth and Thompson escalate the lawsuits to a higher court. Though Ainsworth and Thompson chafed painfully, they ultimately "yielded" to the Ladd brothers' preferences to settle with the outside stockholders out of court for $35,000. A decade later, Ainsworth was still bitter about the compromise, admitting to his children that it had remained "a thorn in the flesh to me, because I knew the community misjudged us."

13

UNBOUNDED EXPANSION

After accomplishing their goal of gaining full control of the OSN, Ainsworth, Thompson, Reed and William reallocated their energies to expanding the company like never before. They more than doubled their capitalization, from $2 million to $5 million; commissioned the construction of a new headquarters building; and completed a 105-mile telegraph line from Portland to The Dalles, the longest yet built in the Pacific Northwest. The first live communication between the two cities was sent over the OSN's wires on June 6, 1868.

Offsetting the board's heavy expenditures on new fixed assets was an impressive business recovery during the second half of 1867. After forming a partnership with a coastal steamship and a stagecoach line to offer the first through service from San Francisco to the Idaho mining districts, a steadier flow of passengers and freight up the Columbia River was established and delivered directly to the OSN's wharf in Portland. Downriver freight traffic increased dramatically during the harvest as a bumper crop in the Walla Walla Valley crammed the company's warehouses, wharves and steamboat decks with wheat and flour shipments bound for export.

In 1868, miners penetrated farther into the western interior, and the OSN followed. The spring rush to Boulder Creek, Montana Territory, drove customers to the company's new fleet operating on such remote inland waterways as Lake Pend Oreille and the Clark Fork River. The following spring, the OSN pushed farther east by partnering with more stagecoach

Above: OSN headquarters between First, Pine and Ash Streets in Portland. The company built the full block in the late 1860s. *Courtesy of University of Oregon.*

Right: The OSN's nine-hundred-foot-long warehouse at Celilo, where wheat cargos were transferred from steamboats to railcars. *Courtesy of Oregon Historical Society.*

lines and inaugurated the first through service to Salt Lake City. By summer, the line was extended to a railroad connection with service to New York.

The board infiltrated other Portland institutions to help protect and advance their expansion plans at the OSN. William was elected chairman of the Board of Trade, where he exercised his power over arbitration case rulings to settle disputes between the OSN and its customers. Thompson became a board member of the Willamette Iron Works, one of the OSN's

Reed befriended Ulysses S. Grant when the two lived near Fort Vancouver before the Civil War. Grant remained in contact with Reed about the OSN's affairs. *Courtesy of Library of Congress.*

most important suppliers, where he could influence the prices the OSN paid for its steamboat and railroad equipment.

Of all the efforts the directors made outside company headquarters to advance the OSN's interests, Reed's work proved to be by far the most impactful. Despite Daniel's lack of confidence in his potential as a political lobbyist, Reed's months in Washington, D.C., proved pivotal for the OSN's future. The earnest and indefatigable Reed immersed himself in his solitary task of winning the support of lawmakers and railroad executives to advance the OSN's expansion. Already an old friend of Ulysses S. Grant—the two had become acquainted when they were living at Fort Vancouver in the early 1850s—Reed developed strategic relationships with Speaker of the House Schuyler Colfax and Congressman Oakes Ames, who was intimately involved in advancing transcontinental railroad interests. Reed worked with Oregon senators George Williams and Henry Corbett to pass three bills to prevent the Washington territorial legislature, longtime enemy of the OSN, from obstructing the company's operations at the Cascades. Reed also employed the assistance of Williams and Corbett to lobby Congress for the appropriation of government funds to remove the John Day rapids so that the company's steamboats could operate year-round above The Dalles.

RAILROAD MANIA

Though Reed chafed under the painfully slow process by which business was conducted in the halls of Congress—complaining to Ainsworth that it took *"forever* to accomplish anything"—Reed's late-night parlor conversations with transcontinental railroad lobbyists proved to be critical in securing the OSN's future. Exposure to ideas and strategies practiced by eastern business owners quickly seduced Reed to the obsession with American railroads gripping capitalists during the first two decades after the Civil War. Reed warned Ainsworth that based on the talk he was hearing from other leaders in the transportation sector, "the days of the

Threshing wheat east of the Cascade Mountains. Shipment of this crop remained the OSN's most lucrative revenue source throughout the 1870s. *Courtesy of Oregon Historical Society.*

Grenville Dodge failed to convince Congress to approve a Union Pacific Railroad connection with the OSN. *Courtesy of Library of Congress.*

supremacy of steamboat navigation on inland waters were numbered." However, Reed assured Ainsworth, given their plans to partner or sell to a transcontinental railroad, he was more convinced than ever of the OSN's future prospects for profit and wealth for the board members. "We are *now* in a position," Reed made clear to Ainsworth, "to make all the money we could reasonably ask."

While in Washington, D.C., Reed cultivated relationships with both the Union Pacific and Northern Pacific Railroad lobbyists. Reed was especially interested in the Union Pacific, judging it to possess "unlimited means" to fund an acquisition of the OSN. In attempting to spark their interest in a partnership with the OSN, Reed shared with the railroad men his predictions of future shipping profits of the burgeoning eastern Washington and Oregon wheat belt, whose output he argued was more impressive than that of the Willamette Valley. Reed was pleasantly surprised that he found attentive audiences when discussing the OSN, updating Ainsworth almost gleefully that not only had eastern capitalists and lawmakers heard about the OSN, but many "put it down as among the big institutions of the country" as well.

Indeed, after Reed returned to Portland, the relationships he established with executives of both the Union Pacific and Northern Pacific led to an exchange of letters and telegrams to discuss a connection with the OSN's line. In January 1868, Union Pacific contact Grenville Dodge made plans to present a bill to Congress requesting funds to extend the railroad north to the Puget Sound and to construct a branch line south to Portland. Dodge also ordered a survey for a branch line to one of the OSN's Snake River steamboat landings.

Meanwhile, Ainsworth courted the Northern Pacific by entertaining visiting executives and engineers on a free tour of the Puget Sound and of the entire OSN line, from Astoria to Montana. The party was so impressed with Ainsworth's hospitality that they wrote a letter of appreciation published in the *Morning Oregonian*. In their report to upper management, Northern Pacific engineers showered Ainsworth and the OSN with flowery praise.

Ultimately, Dodge's bill fell through, and construction of the Union Pacific never turned north from its heading west, where it merged with the Central Pacific's track in 1869. But early the next year, Ainsworth's and Reed's many meetings, talks, letters, telegrams and soirees over the previous four years with railroad executives and their supporters appeared to pay off when Congress amended the Northern Pacific's charter. The government granted the railroad the option to build its main line across the eastern Washington Territory to the Puget Sound or along the Columbia River to Portland. In addition, a new charter was issued to allow the Northern Pacific to construct a branch line connecting the Puget Sound and Portland.

A deal with a transcontinental railroad now seemed inevitable.

THE ACQUISITION

The inevitable did occur in February 1872, when Ainsworth received a telegram from Jay Cooke, owner of the Northern Pacific. Cooke requested a meeting with Ainsworth and Thompson at the railroad's headquarters in New York for the purpose of discussing terms for an acquisition.

Ainsworth and Thompson arrived in New York the next month. As they sat in the elegant lobby of the Northern Pacific's administrative building, the two old friends no doubt reflected on the deeper meaning of the occasion within the context of the previous twelve years they had shared as close business partners. The countless and strenuous hours, financial risks and personal sacrifices that the two men had endured building the OSN's transportation empire seemed to have led up to this moment. If Ainsworth and Thompson could make a deal with Cooke, the two Portlanders anticipated splitting at least $1 million among themselves, Reed and the Ladd brothers. Such a transaction would make them rich, as Ainsworth once wrote of the OSN's first year of profits, "beyond our most sanguine expectations."

Ainsworth and Thompson's excitement waned as they waited an inordinate amount of time in the Northern Pacific's lobby. Thompson grew impatient, then furious, and stormed out of the building. When the railroad executives finally strode into the room to greet the two men, Ainsworth informed them why Thompson was not present. The directors rushed out of the building in search of Thompson and caught up with him on a nearby street. The Northern Pacific executives proffered heartfelt apologies, coaxed him back to the offices and sat down to start the meeting.

After several hours of what Ainsworth later described as "much talk and frequent disagreements," the group reached an impasse, and it appeared as though an agreement would not be possible. The meeting adjourned, and Ainsworth and Thompson began making plans to return to Portland early. They were suddenly interrupted by Northern Pacific director Thomas

Canfield, who convinced the men to cancel their plans and join him for dinner at Cooke's estate, where they would continue negotiations.

At Cooke's obscenely lavish, fifty-three-room, seventy-five-thousand-square-foot mansion outside of Philadelphia, dinner was hosted with Ainsworth and Thompson as guests of honor. Thompson, accustomed to the more direct communication styles of Ainsworth and Reed, chafed at Cooke's aversion to discussing business at dinner and instead filling the time with light conversation about trivial topics. After dinner, the men withdrew to the mansion's library, where Cooke finally resumed negotiations.

In the library, the three men came to a consensus. Ainsworth and Thompson agreed to sell 75 percent of all outstanding OSN stock, at a par value of $1.5 million, half to be paid as cash and the balance as Northern Pacific bonds paying 7 percent interest. As the new majority stockholder, Cooke technically wielded control over company policy, but he allowed all board members to retain their management roles and maintain their control over daily operations. Cooke stood to profit from the lion's share of the OSN's future dividends, but Ainsworth, Thompson, Reed and the Ladd brothers would profit from splitting $750,000 and a total annual interest income of nearly $55,000. Cooke demonstrated his trust in Ainsworth by appointing him managing director of the railroad company's Pacific Coast Division, wherein Ainsworth's principal responsibility would be to fulfill the company's charter for constructing a branch line connecting Portland and the Puget Sound. It was an arrangement that appeared mutually beneficial and stable for both parties.

14

MAYHEM

Ainsworth, Thompson, Reed and the Ladd brothers were more confident than ever in their OSN's future. Shortly after Jay Cooke purchased the majority of the company's stock, the Northern Pacific secured rights-of-way through the Columbia River Gorge in preparation to build its main line down the Oregon shore to Portland. The railroad's branch line from the Puget Sound to Kalama, Washington Territory, already under construction before the deal was made with Cooke, increased the OSN's revenue when its steamboats began shipping materials, equipment, supplies and laborers from Astoria and Portland to the jobsite.

Portland promoters and capitalists were just as excited as the OSN Board of Directors about the acquisition; they viewed the Northern Pacific's plans as a sort of economic salvation. An *Morning Oregonian* journalist described the coming of the railroad as "one of the most important enterprises ever initiated in this or any other country…open(ing) to our immediate view the great future of the Northwest.…One promising greater advantages does not exist." As soon as news spread that the Northern Pacific had chosen Kalama as the terminus for its branch line to the Puget Sound, Portland real estate speculators flocked to the area surrounding the railroad's machine shop and mill, hastily constructing houses and a large hotel.

Outside their new responsibilities to the Northern Pacific, the OSN Board of Directors continued apace with aggressive expansion. Two new stern-wheelers were commissioned in 1871, one of which was the largest yet built by the company, with a total length of 177 feet. To demonstrate their appreciation of Alvinza Heyward's willingness to loan his name in the board's secret plan to trigger the OSN stock panic of 1866, one of the new stern-wheelers was named after Heyward's daughter. In addition to growing its fleet, the board grew its new partnerships with regional stagecoach lines and railroads to break into the Midwest market, creating through services to Chicago and Omaha by way of the Columbia and Snake Rivers. To help offset the cost of these investments, the board cut dividends as much as possible and, one month, paid as little as .25 percent.

The Portland press celebrated the OSN's recent developments and interpreted them as more confirmation of the company's merits. A journalist who traveled the company's new steamboat route to Kalama published a review that read more like advertising copy than an objective narrative, claiming that throughout the OSN's history, it "always had their boats and cars constructed in the very best manner, and in the selection of their officers have taken special pains to secure the services of careful and competent men."

TAKING ENEMY FIRE

Though the OSN's recent accomplishments pleased its supporters, they grated on its old enemies. By the 1870s, complaints from these enemies had grown louder than ever. Business owners at The Dalles continued to wail about the OSN's rates. "We do not believe there is any place in the United States," a journalist at the *Weekly Mountaineer* claimed, "where freights are as high…as on the Columbia River." Reed, who took it upon himself to manage the OSN's public relations, queried a friend living in The Dalles about the area's general mood toward the company. "There is a narrow and contracted deep seated feeling of jealousy and hatred toward the O.S.N. Co.," Reed's correspondent bluntly responded, "and all you can do cannot remove it."

Farther upriver, the smaller, remoter agricultural communities—the most vulnerable to the OSN's high rates—were particularly resentful of the company's rise to power. Journalists in these communities villainized individual members of the OSN Board of Directors. The *Walla Walla Union* berated the company's executives as "the most soulless and little hearted set of monopolists that ever cursed a country." The Baker City *Bedrock Democrat* personally attacked Ainsworth, Reed and William, describing them as "codfish aristocrats…sordid and grasping," reminding readers that

Oregon senator John Mitchell attempted to rally Congress against the OSN and lobbied for the completion of the Cascade Locks and Canal. *Courtesy of Oregon Historical Society.*

they were "poorer than skimmed milk" before they founded the company. Now, "all they had to do was…shovel the gold dust into their coffers." The *Democrat* pulled no punches when criticizing the OSN board, commenting that "superficial, unthinking observers give to them great credit for being sharp financiers. But they are not; they are stupid bunglers."

Prospective competitors capitalized on the climate of discontent east of the Cascade Mountains with direct attacks on the OSN. In 1871, two Portland attorneys, John Mitchell and William Chapman, incorporated the Portland, Dalles and Salt Lake Railroad to construct a line on the Oregon shore of the Columbia. This, the attorneys' second campaign against the OSN, was more formidable than their failed first attempt. Mitchell used his new influence as Oregon senator to gain congressional support for their new company and, after lobbying legislatures, obtained rights-of-way for the proposed railroad. Mitchell was even successful in convincing the State of Oregon to subsidize $3 million in construction expenses. Mitchell and Chapman sold bonds to attempt to cover the balance of the expensive project.

Even though Mitchell and Chapman had obtained legal approval to build most of their railroad, to complete it, they needed to acquire right-of-way through the OSN's property on the Oregon shore of the Cascades. After failing to receive a response from the board after submitting multiple offers to purchase their property, Mitchell and Chapman filed and won a lawsuit against the OSN to purchase right-of-way across its property. The judge ordered the OSN to sell a sixty-five-foot-wide strip of land running the entire length of the Cascades rapids to Mitchell and Chapman for $10,000.

But neither Mitchell nor Chapman possessed enough cash to cover the purchase price. They scrambled to secure a loan but were unsuccessful. Ainsworth was not surprised; he was aware of Chapman's unfavorable reputation in the local business community. "I don't believe he could borrow $50 in Portland without giving security," Ainsworth wrote of Chapman during litigation. "His railroad charter is worth nothing; no intelligent capital can ever be induced to take hold of it...we do not fear him." A desperate Chapman eventually resorted to heartfelt overtures to Portland citizens published in the *Daily Bulletin*. He admitted that his railroad company was short on capital and that "without your assistance, I can carry it no further."

Chapman's pleas were left unanswered. As Ainsworth predicted, he and Mitchell could not raise the $10,000 necessary to purchase the Cascades right-of-way, their case was dismissed and their railroad company disbanded.

THE GREAT DEPRESSION

By August 1873, the Mitchell-Chapman threat had been neutralized and the board had turned its attention to its favorite expansion projects. As construction continued on the Northern Pacific's branch line to the Puget Sound, the OSN continued to collect profits servicing the new passenger and freight trade between Portland and Kalama. The company's newest luxury stern-wheeler was christened in the name of one of Ainsworth's daughters and launched at The Dalles. At 177 feet long, it was the largest steamboat yet to ply the Columbia River above the Cascades.

Then, just when it appeared the OSN had resumed its smooth course of prosperity, the unthinkable blindsided the board: the company's new owner declared bankruptcy.

Jay Cooke's firm, like so many of its peers in the financial sector after the Civil War, made outsized bets on future profits and became overexposed to railroad securities. An economic crisis in Europe during the early 1870s turned foreign investors away from the millions of dollars in Northern Pacific bonds that Cooke's firm was desperately trying to sell to its large clientele overseas, saddling Cooke's firm with more debt than it could possibly service. The firm soon found it could not borrow enough cash to remain solvent. On September 18, Jay Cooke and Company, long viewed as the bellwether of U.S. finance, shocked the American business community when it ushered out its customers and locked its doors during the middle of the day. Word spread rapidly about the event, and panic ensued, triggering runs on banks along the East Coast. In the coming days, several major financial firms across the country met the same fate as Jay Cooke and Company. The momentum continued until, for the first time in its history, the New York Stock Exchange shut its doors and suspended trading.

The economic mayhem that gripped the United States immediately following Cooke's bankruptcy set off a recession of such magnitude that it was referred to as "the Great Depression" for the next fifty-six years, until the stock market crash of 1929 claimed the moniker. For the OSN Board of Directors, the financial catastrophe of 1873 significantly depreciated the value of a large portion of its wealth. The $750,000 in Northern Pacific bonds that the board accepted from Cooke as partial payment for his purchase of OSN stock lost 90 percent of its value, and there was little hope of any of the promised future interest payments. The $1.5 million in OSN shares once owned by Cooke was possessed by his creditors, who listed them on the New York and Philadelphia Stock Exchanges for 86 percent under their par value for the purpose of attracting a quick sale.

Like the future value of the board members' securities, after the panic, the fate of the OSN was rendered uncertain. Legal control of the OSN, once belonging to a single private company with intimate familiarity, appreciation and vested interest in its assets, operations and future, was now for sale and subject to dilution among any number of individual shareholders with limited knowledge or regard for the company.

The fate of the Northern Pacific looked even worse. The collapse of Cooke's firm abruptly shut off the primary source of funding for the railroad. In the absence of available cash, equipment in transport from New York could not be delivered for installation on the branch line from Kalama to the Puget Sound. Exasperated managers immediately halted construction and ordered all workers off the jobsite without pay. The incensed workers became enraged, formed a mob and took armed possession of all Northern Pacific property at Kalama, refusing to leave the premises or allow access to the property until they received their wages in cash.

It was a situation worse than the OSN Board of Directors could have ever imagined.

15

THE CASH CROP

D uring the depression that began in 1873, the still predominantly agrarian Pacific Northwest economy did not suffer as acutely as that of the more industrialized East Coast. Portlanders were relieved, but they were particularly proud of having avoided the financial havoc occurring in San Francisco. Amid the depression, a *Morning Oregonian* journalist allowed Portland business owners permission to "congratulate themselves" in practicing restraint and investing in conservative equities instead of the highly speculative and risky securities that brought down William Ralston's Bank of California. "Our banks," the Portland journalist huffed, "move on the even tenor of their way attending to their legitimate commercial transactions." Another writer warned readers that there was a lesson in the fate of the Bank of California: "If Oregonians insisted on investing in banks, let them be banks owned and operated by Oregonians."

Notwithstanding its exposure to Jay Cooke's bankruptcy, the OSN pulled through the ordeal largely unfazed. If anything, the crisis presented rare opportunities for which the board was positioned to take full advantage. Because the OSN carried no debt and maintained such a large surplus of cash on hand, it was able to issue loans to struggling Portland firms and enjoy income from interest payments. Two years into the depression, the board extended a $50,000 loan to the Ladd brothers' bank at 6 percent interest, adding $3,000 per month to the OSN's surplus.

Though the company clearly had cash, the board hid the good health of the OSN's financial condition from individuals the board distrusted. When Cooke, desperate to recover the value of his large lot of OSN shares, asked Ainsworth to raise dividends to make the stock more attractive to East Coast investors, Ainsworth responded that the company could not afford to do so. Meanwhile, as prices fluctuated downward on the New York Stock Exchange, John Ladd quietly purchased small amounts of OSN shares on the board's behalf.

In Portland, Ainsworth, Thompson and Reed took charge of salvaging the OSN's vital connection with the Northern Pacific Railroad. When work on the branch line to the Puget Sound abruptly stopped, only half of the railroad was completed, and the government charter authorizing construction was scheduled to expire in less than two years. Northern Pacific executives did not appear to have plans to finish the line in time, and the project seemed doomed to fail. Superseding the railroad's board, Ainsworth, Thompson and Reed took control of the branch line. They combined their personal funds and paid for the remaining $60,000 in delivery fees due to complete the shipment of rails to the construction site at Kalama. Next, Ainsworth traveled to Kalama, where he confronted the mob of idle workers standing guard over the Northern Pacific property. In what Ainsworth described as a "protracted conference" that lasted long after nightfall, he negotiated with the crowd of disgruntled men until an agreement was made. In exchange for their promises to peacefully vacate the premises, Ainsworth agreed to pay the laborers half their due wages and sign their paychecks so that they could be reimbursed for the remainder. After the mob evacuated, Ainsworth, Thompson and Reed hired a new crew and supervised the laying of approximately twelve miles of track to finish the branch line to the Puget Sound. The laborers finished the job with less than twenty-four hours to spare before the charter was due to expire.

COMPLETING THE FLEET

After regular train service between Kalama and the Puget Sound began in 1875, Ainsworth, Thompson and Reed refocused their attention on the OSN, launching the most aggressive expansion campaign in the company's history.

Increased wheat production across eastern Oregon and the Washington Territory overwhelmed the OSN's system, rendering its facilities insufficient.

More and larger steamboats, warehouses and wharves were needed to accommodate the influx of freight. "It will be our policy," Reed promised a farmer living in the remote riverside settlement of Grange City, "to keep our improvements and facilities fully up with the growth of the country." In September 1875, the board committed to a wholesale upgrade of its line and ordered the refurbishment of four steamboats, two barges, its wharf at Umatilla and its warehouse and wharf in Portland and the purchase of three new steamboats.

Three months later, the board aggressively expanded the OSN's wheat shipping business, now its most significant revenue source, by purchasing the Willamette Transportation and Locks Company and the Astoria Farmers Company. The acquisitions gave the OSN control of the Willamette River wheat trade as far upriver as Eugene City and as far west as Astoria, where the commodity would be delivered, stored and loaded onto ocean ships bound for export markets. The absorption of competitors' assets added seven steamboats and three barges to the OSN's fleet, a navigation lock at Oregon City and warehouses, wharves and prime waterfront real estate at Astoria. By 1876, with the exception of two independently owned stern-wheelers, every steam-powered vessel in service on the Columbia, Snake and Willamette Rivers was now controlled by the OSN.

But the OSN Board of Directors was far from finished with expanding its fleet. Between 1876 and 1878, the OSN built a total of ten new steamboats. The company's shipyard at Celilo produced the first six stern-wheelers of the construction spree to meet the urgent demand for wheat transport upriver. With light drafts and tonnage, these vessels were specifically designed to navigate the upper reaches of the Columbia and Snake Rivers and their tributaries with heavy loads of freight.

The remaining four steamboats commissioned by the OSN in the late 1870s proved to be the crowning achievements of the company's career in shipbuilding and earned the vessels special places in maritime history as some of the best examples of steamboat construction produced on the West Coast. These stern-wheelers, unlike the OSN's freight fleet above Celilo, were designed with what Thompson described as "first class" accommodations that surpassed any other watercraft on the Columbia and Willamette Rivers.

Passenger comfort and safety were the board's priorities for this luxury fleet, and no expense was spared in equipping the steamers with the most modern luxury accouterments and mechanical equipment. All four stern-wheelers featured elaborate moldings and paneling on their exterior

The *R.R. Thompson* was one of the OSN's largest and most luxurious stern-wheelers. *Courtesy of Multnomah County Library.*

bulkheads and the interior cabin comforts of a trendy Victorian parlor, such as patterned carpets, detailed trim painting, inlaid carvings, plush leather furniture, brass fixtures, chandeliers, marble countertops, giant plate-glass mirrors and spacious staterooms. To maximize cruising comfort, the hulls were designed with a much larger size and heavier weight than the typical stern-wheeler. When completed, three of the four steamers measured at least two hundred feet in length.

At 246 feet long, the *Wide West* was not only the largest of the OSN's luxury stern-wheelers but was also the most technologically advanced. In the pilothouse, the *Wide West* featured a hydraulic steering system, rendering the traditional towering wheel obsolete and allowing the enormous stern-wheeler's course to be controlled by the light touch of a small lever. In the passenger cabin, toilets were plumbed with running water to increase sanitation. Below decks in the engine room, a sectional boiler with a cutoff mechanism was installed to increase fuel efficiency. The board spent a total of $114,000 in constructing the *Wide West*, more than it invested in any river vessel throughout the company's entire history.

To help increase the odds of a return on this investment, the board made a grand effort to advertise the launching of its new luxury stern-

Passenger cabin on the *S.G. Reed*, one of the OSN's "first class" stern-wheelers. *Author's collection.*

Advertising illustration of the ladies' cabin on the *R.R. Thompson*. *Author's collection.*

wheelers. Before construction was finished, OSN chief engineer John Gates was sent by the board to interview with the *Morning Oregonian*, where he laid out the blueprints of each steamboat for reporters and answered questions about their specifications. The reporters later compared notes and declared to the Portland public that they had just seen the makings of "the most magnificent fleet of river steamers of any corporation on the Pacific Coast." After the *Wide West* was launched, the board turned its first cruise into an exclusive publicity event in which journalists and photographers attended as honored guests. After the giant steamer left the Portland wharf, the party gathered in the dining saloon and sat down to a spread of expensive foods and wine carefully selected by Reed, who leveraged his political skills to charm the guests as host. Glowing reviews of the OSN's "perfect floating palaces" appeared in local newspapers following the cruise.

OLD ENEMIES, NEW CHALLENGES

As the power of the OSN monopoly strengthened throughout the late 1870s, so did the forces against it.

The growing population of farmers settling in the Pacific Northwest interior increased the local influence of the Granger movement, which spread from the Midwest to the West Coast. The movement's platform against capitalist corporations and their negative impacts on America's small agricultural operations resonated with Northwest farmers and increased the number of complaints published about the OSN.

Reed, in charge of the company's public relations, tried in vain to dispel the grievances. In a long letter to Harvey Scott, *Morning Oregonian* editor, Reed vehemently objected to the popular opinion that the OSN was taking advantage of the region's farmers by charging exorbitant freight rates. He attempted to persuade readers by presenting an exhaustive breakdown of how the costs of freight shipping on the Columbia River justified the OSN's current rates and pointed out how much more California transportation companies charged their customers.

The crescendo of complaints about the OSN finally captured the attention of lawmakers in Washington, D.C. In the early 1870s, government funds were allocated to address these complaints and, for the first time in history, initiate a permanent solution to the transportation bottleneck caused by the Cascades rapids. Army Corps of Engineers surveyors were

Cascade Locks and Canal under construction, 1880s. Congress approved this $4 million project to break the OSN's monopoly. *Courtesy of Oregon Historical Society.*

dispatched to the Cascades, where they performed a feasibility study for the construction of a shipping canal and navigation lock to bypass the entire six miles of rapids. Contrary to preliminary estimates of around $1 million, the government survey found that the canal and locks could be constructed with a budget of as little as $300,000.

Senator James Mitchell, who with William Chapman failed twice in his campaigns to break up the OSN's monopoly in local courts, continued to leverage his presence in Congress to challenge the company. In 1878, Mitchell launched his third assault on the OSN by delivering a speech to the Senate titled, "The Columbia River, Its Freedom Must Be Established, the Monopoly of the Oregon Steam Navigation Co. Must Be Broken, the Canal and Locks at the Cascades Must Be Completed." Mitchell used this platform to present a bill to incorporate a competing line from Portland to The Dalles.

The OSN Board of Directors avoided the expense of battling Mitchell in court a third time when his latest venture quickly ended in failure. A more daunting battle against the U.S. government still loomed on the horizon, one that the board realized it could not fight with any hope of winning. In 1877, resigned to the increasing likelihood that the Army Corps of Engineers would commandeer its land at the Cascades to construct a canal and locks, the board ordered all refurbishments and ongoing maintenance on the Oregon portage discontinued. Intimately familiar with the political machinations of Washington, D.C., Reed cheerfully reassured Thompson that all was not lost if the government condemned their property. Reed argued that the OSN was "*certainly* in as good a shape as we possibly could be to put in a *big* claim for damages" and that the government would be forced to compensate the OSN for the imposition.

While the board successfully avoided two potentially expensive battles in the late 1870s, a third appeared to be unavoidable. At stake was the most significant source of the company's profit, so victory was critical to the OSN's future, regardless of the cost of the fight. The battle would be intense, but it would be the last the OSN Board of Directors would be forced to fight.

16

THE FINAL BATTLE

Thanks to John Ladd's diligent monitoring of the price quotes of OSN shares on the New York Stock Exchange, the board was able to purchase the company's stock each time it fell to record-low prices. After five years of such purchases, John had reclaimed every OSN share from Jay Cooke's creditors. By 1878, the board had regained its previous control over the OSN's stock and had paid 75 percent under par value while doing so.

Though it had reclaimed control over its company, the OSN board had changed dramatically since making the deal with Cooke. In 1877, after seventeen years of service, Thompson resigned and returned to California, where he built a large mansion in the center of Alameda and started his next venture, improving the community's freshwater system. John Sprague, Ainsworth's fellow board member at the Northern Pacific and William Ladd's confidant on Portland's Board of Trade, was elected to fill Thompson's seat.

Though he had moved on from the OSN, his old friends Ainsworth and Reed called on Thompson and his patient, deliberate and calming demeanor for key reinforcement in the final battle the board waged to win complete control of the Columbia River.

The board's opponent for its final battle proved to be a formidable enemy, or, as Ainsworth described them, "the toughest nut we had to crack." This, one of the OSN's oldest enemies, had waged a rate war against the larger company's steamboat service in the early 1860s but was forced to surrender, sparking a resentment that lasted over a decade. Like the OSN itself, its last enemy used a conservative approach to finances and turned a small and underfunded transportation enterprise into a highly profitable and strategically valuable operation that played an integral role in the shipping of one of the Pacific Northwest's most valuable exports.

In his opponent, Ainsworth met his equal in intelligence, perseverance and unyielding negotiation skills. "He was a man of brains," Ainsworth once admitted of his adversary. "He was very ambitious to succeed in everything he undertook."

THE PRIZE

At stake was the Walla Walla and Columbia River Railroad, a forty-six-mile, narrow-gauge track that connected the steamboat landing at Wallula to Walla Walla, Washington Territory. Construction began in 1872, and in spite of significant material shortages, planning complications and financial setbacks, the railroad was not only completed but it also became the primary means of wheat transport from the Walla Walla valley to the Columbia River, replacing the long and difficult wagon road that wound through the sandy landscape.

Though the railroad had earned an unflattering reputation as possessing subpar facilities—decommissioned boxcars outfitted with benches served as passenger cars—the line became a key link in the Pacific Northwest wheat trade and thus the OSN's business. The railroad's early investors accurately predicted that regional wheat farming would continue to expand and harvests would eventually replace gold and silver as the interior Northwest's most valuable commodity. By the late 1870s, such large quantities of wheat were pouring out of the Walla Walla valley that during the harvest, the railroad's trains were kept in motion all hours of the day hauling sacks to the OSN's wharves and warehouses at Wallula.

Both the owners of the Walla Walla and Columbia River Railroad and the OSN Board of Directors understood that the railroad, in supplying most of the freight for the OSN's steamboats upriver, controlled a significant portion of the larger company's business. Because of their established service to Wallula, shipping via the OSN was a natural choice. But, if the railroad owners desired, they could feasibly build their own wharves, warehouses and steamboats to compete against the OSN and even control the Columbia River wheat trade.

Neutralizing the looming threat that the railroad could, at will, remove a critical link in the OSN's most important transportation chain and use it against it became the board's highest priority. To Ainsworth, the scenario would inevitably become a reality. "It was evident that [the railroad] would take the first opportunity to hit us," Ainsworth described his nervous mood about the matter. "It was only a question of a very short time." Since building a competing railroad would require significant financial outlay and risk, the OSN leaders determined to employ their usual strategy of purchasing their competition. To initiate negotiations, Ainsworth wrote to the railroad's founder, owner and general manager, Dorsey Baker.

In Battle

Known locally as "Doc" because of his brief stint in the medical profession, Baker entered the transportation industry in 1862, when he helped found the People's Transportation Company. Baker lost most of his investment— and personal fortune—when, after a brief but intense rate war with the OSN, the business suffered a crippling blow to its capital, forcing him and his partners to sell their steamboats and disband. A few years later, Baker again challenged the OSN's monopoly by attempting to construct a railroad on the north shore of the Cascades. Before he could make any tangible progress, he was again thwarted by the larger company. Baker then took his railroad ambitions upriver to Walla Walla.

Unsurprisingly, after he received Ainsworth's letter inquiring about the purchase of his railroad, Baker neglected to respond. Ainsworth persisted. He attempted the more aggressive strategy of dispatching new OSN board member John Sprague to Walla Walla to track down Baker and attempt in-person negotiations. In Walla Walla, Sprague eventually found Baker and sat down with him to discuss the purchase of his railroad, but Baker remained "very stiff" and refused to name a price. Frustrated, Sprague returned to Portland.

Undeterred, Ainsworth raised the stakes by orchestrating a ruse to induce Baker to sell. Ainsworth proposed to the OSN board that it authorize the purchase of materials for constructing a railroad comparable to Baker's and ship them to Wallula. Ainsworth predicted that on learning of the OSN's construction materials at Wallula, Baker would realize a railroad war with the OSN would be imminent and that his business was not likely to survive another competition with the larger company, and he therefore would become more amenable to selling. The board approved Ainsworth's plan and immediately moved to purchase all the components of a new railroad, including thirty-five miles of rails, two locomotives and fittings for twenty freight cars.

Ainsworth's ruse proved effective. After hearing about the OSN's order for railroad materials, Baker traveled to Portland. He appeared at the OSN's headquarters, met with Ainsworth and requested a resumption of negotiations. Ainsworth agreed and asked Reed and Thompson to attend the proceedings.

The negotiation itself proved to be the most arduous aspect of the OSN's final battle. Meetings dragged on for hours as the stubborn Baker, conflicted and reluctant to relinquish control of the most successful business venture of his career and its sizeable dividend income, refused to cede points to the OSN team. Late into the evening, the exasperated group adjourned and made plans to reconvene the next day.

Tense discussions continued for four more days; each evening the group reached a frustrating impasse. "We have been 'wrestling' with Dr Baker…night and day," an exhausted Reed updated Ainsworth about the negotiations, "and *we* have had a hell of a time." By the end of the sixth day

The *D.S. Baker* shooting the Cascade rapids. It was one of the last steamboats constructed by the OSN. *Courtesy of Multnomah County Library.*

of the negotiation, the group had finally reached an agreement. Finding Baker wholly unwilling to give up complete control of his railroad, the OSN team backed down, agreed to allow him to retain one-sixth ownership and paid $433,000 for the remainder of the railroad's stock.

The OSN emerged victorious in its battle for control of the Walla Walla and Columbia River Railroad, but Baker also enjoyed a victory. The price the OSN paid for his railroad far exceeded the original cost of its construction, producing a sizeable profit for Baker and his investors. Baker recovered his lost fortune, and his railroad made history by connecting the isolated frontier community directly to Columbia River commerce. In holding fast to his interests and rendering himself a difficult target for the OSN board, Baker exacted his revenge on an enemy that years before had nearly ruined his financial health and business prospects.

The OSN paid homage to its most formidable opponent by naming its next steamboat after Baker's son.

17

END OF THE LINE

Ainsworth began the year 1879 both physically and mentally exhausted.

Prone to migraines throughout most of his career, the fifty-six-year-old found himself suffering from more bodily illnesses, anxiety and depression than ever before as he struggled to keep up with the daily management of both the OSN and the Northern Pacific's regional operations. "My cares," a despondent Ainsworth candidly wrote to his family about his declining condition, "multiply so rapidly, and health giving way more and more." For the first time in his nineteen years at the OSN, Ainsworth's physical condition prevented him from attending a board meeting.

In addition to feeling sick and overwhelmed at work, Ainsworth also felt lost. With Thompson retired and Reed on an extended vacation overseas, Ainsworth acted alone in making strategic decisions and realized how much he depended on his two most trusted partners for managerial and emotional support. He lamented to his family, "I miss the council of my associates, Thompson and Reed, very much." A desperate Ainsworth admitted to his children that he felt "at times like giving up altogether."

But Ainsworth could not afford to give up. In June, he was presented with the most significant opportunity of his lifetime: an offer to purchase the OSN. Without anyone around him he could trust, Ainsworth saw no choice but to summon what perseverance and stamina he had left to execute the transaction on his own. After its completion, Ainsworth partnered with Reed, his only remaining ally at the OSN, to close one of the largest and most powerful businesses in the nineteenth-century Pacific Northwest.

The Buyout

After negotiating the sale of the OSN to New York capitalist Henry Villard for $5 million, Ainsworth's next hurdle was finalizing the contract. Villard's attorney drafted an agreement and presented it to Ainsworth, but the OSN's attorney resigned just a few days before, leaving the company without expert consultation necessary to legally protect its interests. Anxious to return to New York with the contract in hand, Villard set tight deadlines for his legal team and with Ainsworth to settle the document's terms.

Without sufficient time to canvas Portland for a trustworthy replacement attorney, Ainsworth took on the task of performing the contract review himself. After poring over legal literature and finding Villard's contract language wanting, Ainsworth returned it to Villard's attorney for revisions. A second draft was produced, but Ainsworth was still dissatisfied. Having lost confidence in Villard's legal team and with less than twenty-four hours before his scheduled meeting with Villard, Ainsworth decided to rewrite the entire contract himself. He worked all day and through the night to finish the document, which included explicit language to protect the OSN board members and stockholders. After their review the next morning, Villard and his attorney accepted and signed Ainsworth's contract.

Ainsworth had good reason for distrusting Villard's contract language. Though he appreciated Villard's plans for the OSN, Ainsworth was skeptical of Villard's means. After making their deal, Villard admitted to Ainsworth that he was "hard run for money just now" and could afford to cover only half of the $100,000 purchase deposit. After he and his attorney returned to New York, Villard secured the balance of the deposit and the $1.9 million he promised Ainsworth in their negotiation but, short of cash, financed it by mortgaging the OSN's stock. Villard's lender, the Farmers' Loan and Trust Company, took possession of the OSN shares and stipulated that it would not turn them over to Villard until he could pay off a percentage of the mortgage. To meet his minimum monthly payments, Villard tapped the OSN's revenue.

Such a leveraged buyout was commonplace among Villard's peers on Wall Street, but to the financially conservative OSN Board of Directors, the arrangement looked risky and appeared to possess all the forebodings of the disaster that had ruined Jay Cooke. Charles Tilton, the OSN's longtime banker and partner of the Ladd brothers, expressed an outright distrust of Villard. "All there is to him," Tilton grumbled to William, "is Wind." Nevertheless, Tilton admitted, Villard's offer was attractive, and it was the only such opportunity the board had entertained for several years. "We must make some Money out of this," he resolved, "for we may not get another so good a thing."

Windbag or not, Villard's record as an international securities broker proved that unlike other potential OSN competitors, he possessed the ability to raise more than enough capital to fund the establishment of a viable competing line on the Columbia River, if he or his wealthy partners in Europe so desired. As ever, it was this risk of competition that Ainsworth feared the most.

NEW MANAGEMENT

News of the OSN's buyout spread rapidly throughout Portland and set the business community abuzz. In local newspapers, reactions spanned a wide spectrum, from celebratory to ominous. The *Morning Oregonian* both applauded Villard's plans for the OSN as a windfall for the Pacific Northwest economy and simultaneously prophesied a calamitous cutoff of trade with the East, citing a rumored silent partnership with the infamous Jay Gould.

In fact, Villard incorporated the Oregon Railway and Navigation Company (OR&N) to serve as a legal receptacle for his purchases of the OSN and other Pacific Northwest transportation businesses. Through the consolidation of these companies, Villard sought to eliminate the destructive effects of competition among them and expand and improve—or as he described it, "harmonize"—every railroad and steamship operation from the Puget Sound to Northern California. Villard, like Reed and Ainsworth, envisioned Portland as the future center of regional trade, and his ultimate goal was to connect the city more directly to East Coast commerce via a transcontinental railroad connection.

Instead of hiring staff in New York to manage his new properties in the Pacific Northwest, Villard deferred to local experts already in the field. He turned first to Ainsworth and Reed for the continued management of the OSN's operation, at least until Villard paid down enough of his mortgage to take control of the stock and reorganize the company's assets for the OR&N's purposes. Ainsworth and Reed agreed, and just a few weeks after the close of the OSN sale, they were elected as directors of the OR&N, under Villard as president.

Reed immediately got to work helping Villard pay off his mortgage by reducing the OSN's recurring expenses. Reed made servicing the OSN's

An OR&N fractional bond. Henry Villard found a ready market for such securities in 1879, but demand disappeared a few years later. *Author's collection.*

$150,000 debt his first priority. During the first month of his new role, Reed reduced the balance by over 40 percent. By the second month, he had eliminated another 27 percent. Villard was pleased, praising Reed for his characteristic earnestness: "You certainly have taken hold of our affairs in a very energetic manner," Villard wrote Reed from New York. By the end of the year, the OSN's only liabilities were $15,000 worth of uncollected bills, claims and judgments. Meanwhile, Villard was able to draw more than anticipated from especially high seasonal increases in freight revenue; the 1879 harvest supplied an average of 150 tons of wheat per day for transport over the company's newly purchased Walla Walla and Columbia River Railroad.

Despite the positive rapport that had been established between the old and new managers of the OSN and their shared visions for the future of Pacific Northwest transportation, it was not long before Villard's naively optimistic and liberal policy began to clash with Ainsworth and Reed's cautious and conservative approach. Just three months after negotiating the sale of the OSN, Ainsworth and Reed were outraged to learn that, without their knowledge, Villard had dispatched his lead engineer to perform a survey of the Oregon shore of the Columbia River from The Dalles to Portland in preparation for constructing a railroad connecting the two cities. Ainsworth and Reed, who first read about the survey in the Portland newspapers, found themselves in the same position where they had put the Cascades portage owners over a decade earlier: outside the inner circle of their own management team.

Reed began writing angry letters to Villard's management team in New York, protesting with arguments and tones remarkably similar to those Daniel Bradford had used with Reed in 1866, when the OSN Board of Directors withheld financial data from him. "It is very annoying to us," Reed wrote, referring to his and Ainsworth's ignorance of Villard's secret plans, "who are supposed to know something about these matters…[and] have large interests." Reed made clear, in his usual blunt style, that he and Ainsworth did not believe the OR&N was yet in the financial condition to fund construction of a one-hundred-mile railroad through the Columbia River Gorge. "What is the use," Reed challenged Villard's inner circle, "of running lines all over the country, and setting every body by the ears, when there is hardly a *possibility* of…building a road for a long time to come[?]… Cannot this be stopped[?]"

In his correspondence directly with Villard, Ainsworth diplomatically warned his boss about the dangers of neglecting to consult himself and Reed when making such large-scale policy decisions regarding local projects: "Things look differently from this stand point from what they do in Wall Street." In his private letters to his family, Ainsworth was much more candid in expressing his feelings about Villard and his tendency to ignore the West Coast management team. Ainsworth claimed Villard "never asked for advice" from himself or Reed, who, unlike Villard, he pointed out, possessed a "large experience, with a record of success as an endorsement." After working for him for several months, Ainsworth judged Villard to be "a good man, of noble impulses and generous disposition," but that he ultimately did not possess the leadership skills Ainsworth felt were necessary to manage companies or capital. Ainsworth wrote that he was most alarmed about Villard's "theory of *one man power*," which he predicted would lead to Villard's ultimate downfall.

CLOSING DOWN

When a new competitor threatened to construct its own line through the Columbia River Gorge, Ainsworth and Reed grew anxious about the potential threat and eventually came around to Villard's idea of building the OR&N railroad connecting The Dalles and Portland, if only for the purpose of avoiding the possibility of starting a war with a competitor.

But Ainsworth continued to nurse serious concerns about Villard's policy decisions and leadership style. Both his satisfaction with his new role and his health continued to decline. By the end of 1879, after having worked for Villard for less than six months, Ainsworth realized that he "wanted to get out of the harness" that he felt Villard placed on him. When Villard asked him to serve another term, Ainsworth refused. In January 1880, Ainsworth attended the OSN's twentieth annual stockholder meeting, at which he presented his formal resignation. The board members, who had been aware of Ainsworth's intent to leave for some time, were not surprised and thanked him affectionately for his two decades of service.

Ainsworth's twenty-seven-year-old son, George, was elected to fill his father's open seat on the OSN board. The younger Ainsworth led the board meetings and supervised the operations of the OSN during its final months of existence, ordering the retrofitting of The Dalles–Celilo railroad for standard-gauge track in preparation for its connection with the OR&N railroad, coordinating the final call for and payment of customer claims and declaring the last dividend payment.

By summer, Villard had gained control of the OSN stock formerly held by his lender and officially unincorporated the company. Nothing significant changed about the former company's fixed assets, which were placed under the management of the OR&N's Columbia and Willamette River Division. Meanwhile, Villard purchased over three hundred acres in southeast Portland to establish the terminus of the OR&N railroad, extended the former Walla Walla and Columbia River Railroad farther east and launched a new ocean steamship for service in the coastal trade.

EPILOGUE

After resigning from both the OSN and OR&N, Ainsworth, now a millionaire, returned to the place where he had started his long and prosperous career in the West with just nine dollars in his pocket. He purchased a fifteen-acre ranch in Oakland, California's Temescal neighborhood, a new, wealthy suburb. At the center of the ranch, Ainsworth constructed a sprawling mansion and surrounded it with an oversized greenhouse, rock grottos, large gardens, carriage houses, barns and a guesthouse. Ainsworth named his estate Roselawn, for his garden's extensive rose collection.

Although he claimed to have chosen California to spend his retirement because of the restorative effects of its more moderate climate, it was likely not a coincidence that Ainsworth built his new home just a few miles from his longtime friend, Robert Thompson, who had relocated to Alameda in 1878. As some of the wealthiest members of their new communities, Ainsworth and Thompson enjoyed all the coveted privileges and notoriety of the Victorian upper class. They hosted and attended glamorous, exclusive and expensive parties; vacationed often; participated in hobbies such as rare art and flower collecting; and were interviewed often by local newspapers regarding their views on public policy.

Ainsworth and Thompson remained active in business and launched many new ventures, especially in banking, transportation and public works. They collaborated on their largest project in retirement: the construction of the first luxury hotel at Redondo Beach. Outside of their business responsibilities,

Ainsworth and Thompson became heavily involved in philanthropy, serving on nonprofit boards and donating to and even founding organizations that supported education and underprivileged groups.

Unlike Ainsworth and Thompson, Reed and William Ladd remained in Portland after the OSN disbanded. Reed invested his fortune in various local businesses such as mines, foundries, railroads and, most famously, agricultural operations. William continued to manage his banking interests, which made up the majority of his personal fortune. Throughout the 1880s, Reed and William grew closer than ever. They bonded over their shared passion for farming and incorporated the Ladd and Reed Farm Company, which served less as a business venture aimed at making profits and more as an outlet for the two friends to indulge in their interest in livestock breeding.

Declining health from various age-related ailments overtook Ainsworth, Reed and William in the early 1890s, forcing them to withdraw from their very active lifestyles. Ainsworth and William died in 1893, and Reed succumbed two years later. Ainsworth and Reed each left their heirs estates worth over $3 million. William, whose portfolio included downtown Portland real estate and a large stake in the bank he owned with his brother John, bequeathed an estate worth $14 million.

Thompson outlived the other OSN board members by over a decade. In 1908, he died at his new mansion in the San Francisco suburbs at the age of eighty-eight. Ever the land speculator, Thompson continued to purchase properties, even when he was infirm, two years before his death. Like Ainsworth and Reed, Thompson left his family $3 million, most of which was retained in his extensive commercial real estate portfolio.

Jacob Kamm, Ainsworth's oldest friend, was the last surviving founder of the OSN. After resigning in 1867, Kamm, like his peers on the OSN Board of Directors, remained active in business until just a few years before his death, investing in mining, real estate and, especially, steamboats. Though Kamm enjoyed an elevated position in Portland society as a member of its small group of wealthy capitalists, unlike his former fellow members of the board, Kamm did not command the respect of his community in his later years. His involvement in many lawsuits, his repeated complaints to public officials about taxes and, even after repeated requests from civic leaders, his refusal to upgrade or even repair his commercial properties in downtown Portland painted Kamm as a curmudgeonly, unapproachable and undesirable figure in the press.

Whereas Reed and Ladd had farming and Ainsworth had gardening, Kamm's expensive retirement hobby was steamboats. He spent thousands of dollars of his own funds on maintaining his favorite vessels, even when dismantling them and building replacements made more financial sense. On the morning of his death in 1912, it was reported that Kamm passed away at his mansion on Fourteenth Street minutes after hearing the departure whistle of his favorite stern-wheeler when it pushed back from the Portland wharf.

THREE YEARS AFTER HE predicted that Villard's lack of experience and competence would cause him to "meet with heavy reverses," Ainsworth was proven correct. After unincorporating the OSN, Villard charged ahead with his hyper-aggressive expansion plans, constructing expensive fixed assets, forming new companies, purchasing competitors and breaking into new markets. His largest acquisition was the struggling Northern Pacific Railroad, which Villard funded by receiving over $20 million in subscriptions from his large client base on Wall Street and in Europe in exchange for equity in his many newly formed holding companies. Once the Northern Pacific was in his control, Villard invested and borrowed

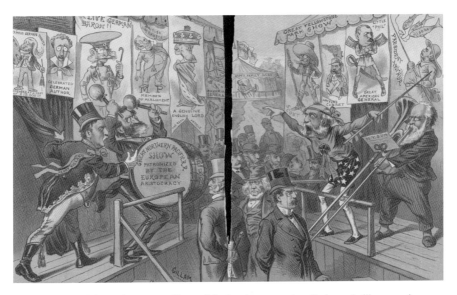

Henry Villard (*left*) was lampooned by political satire magazine *Puck* as a belligerent circus hawker of Northern Pacific Railroad stock. *Courtesy of Library of Congress.*

heavily to complete the unfinished railroad, using his companies' quickly dwindling cash reserves. Villard was successful in accomplishing his vision of completing the first transcontinental railroad to the Pacific Northwest—from Saint Paul, Minnesota, to Portland—but in doing so, he had incurred astronomical amounts of debt, could not borrow the funds desperately needed to cover daily operational costs, witnessed the price of the stocks and bonds of his new companies plummet and was forced to resign from the management of all of his business ventures, including the Northern Pacific and OR&N.

To Ainsworth, Villard's meteoric rise and fall validated his concerns and served as an invaluable lesson for his children. He made clear his disapproval of Villard's behaviors and how much he wished his children would avoid imitating them in a long letter he wrote to his children at the end of his life: "[Villard] has ruined hundreds, if not thousands, who trusted his word and were deceived….Poverty, and even oblivion, with honesty, is infinitely better than Mr. Villard's butterfly history."

IN 1885, THE OR&N, now under new management but still suffering financially, retained twenty-three of the twenty-six steamboats it had purchased from the OSN in 1879. The fleet remained integral to the OR&N's Columbia and Snake River operations, though primarily as a seasonal auxiliary service, taking on extra freight when wheat harvests from the interior overtaxed the company's railroads and accommodating the growing summer vacation trade to southwest Washington and northwest Oregon beaches.

By the turn of the century, nearly all of the original OSN steamboats had been scrapped or wrecked. Some, including the company's masterpiece stern-wheeler, the *Wide West*, were dismantled and their components reused in the construction of new vessels.

The last surviving OSN steamboat, the *Harvest Queen*, ended its unprecedented forty-eight-year career on the Columbia in 1926. After surviving trips down both The Dalles narrows and Cascades rapids, it served in the passenger, freight and towboat trades and, after 1900, was often seen hauling ocean vessels between Portland and Astoria.

When it powered down its engines for the last time in 1927, it marked the end to the OSN's presence on the Columbia River.

The *Harvest Queen*, the last surviving OSN steamboat, laying over at Multnomah Falls during an excursion in the early 1900s. *Courtesy of Oregon Historical Society.*

AINSWORTH AND THOMPSON FELT justified in eliminating anyone who opposed their plans for the OSN and were convinced that in doing so they were fulfilling their duty of protecting the future of the company and its stockholders. The controversial management practices of the OSN board—monopolizing its industry, impeding competition and withholding critical company information from stockholders to advance secret agendas—though illegal and viewed as highly corrupt today, were both legal and commonplace in American business throughout most of the nineteenth century. The corporate expansion stimulus policy of the Lincoln administration did not obligate organizations like the OSN to adhere to standards of trade or responsibility to stockholders, leaving such questions to the discretion of company leaders. Many large post-

Civil War corporations, most notably Credit Mobilier and the Union Pacific Railroad, took advantage of the generous policy governing private companies for more nefarious motives, triggering widespread public criticism and lawsuits that escalated and remained integral to populist politics throughout the remainder of the century.

It was not until a full decade after the disbanding of the OSN that such pressure for lawmakers to regulate trade and hold corporations accountable to their stockholders took purchase, rendering many of the OSN's practices illegal. The first legislation protecting free trade went into effect in 1890 with the passage of the Sherman Act, which outlawed the "restraint" of competition and monopolization. The act was expanded in 1914 with the creation of the Federal Trade Commission (FTC) and the passage of the Clayton Act.

Congress finally began to address the stock manipulation tactics practiced by Ainsworth, Thompson and Reed in 1934, half a century after the OSN existed. Reprioritized after the stock market crash of 1929, insider trading and the withholding of pertinent company financial information were outlawed with the passage of Securities Exchange Commission (SEC) legislation.

TODAY, THERE ARE NO physical relics of the OSN's transportation system left in view on the landscape it once dominated. The Columbia, Snake and Willamette River shorelines are hardly recognizable compared to their appearances in the 1870s. Gone forever are the rapids where the steamboats plied—inundated by dams—and the topography of the land once occupied by the company's railroads and commercial buildings has changed dramatically to accommodate highways and other modern infrastructure projects.

But one can find other relics of the OSN if one looks deeper within the landscape. In the large and small riverside towns throughout the Pacific Northwest, the names of the OSN's board members, steamboats, railroads and other assets can be seen in print. Some are as obvious as the names of neighborhoods, public parks, colleges and the towns themselves. Others are much more subtle; the name of a side street, hotel room or small island. In these relics, etched on paper, plastic, wood and stone, the OSN lives.

The collections of ephemera digitally and physically stored at museums and colleges across the United States contain the most vivid relics of the OSN. The photographs, maps, advertisements, certificates, contracts, personal correspondence, diaries, notes and records contained in these files provide intimate looks into the daily activities of the OSN and the lives of the people connected with the company. For the alert and imaginative interpreter, these documents are a portal into the world of the Northwest's first capitalistic enterprise.

BIBLIOGRAPHY

Manuscripts and Documents

Biographical Sketch of John C. Ainsworth Prepared By Mrs. Frances Fuller Victor, P-A, 72: 3, Bancroft Selections, The Bancroft Library, University of California, Berkeley. Berkeley, California. https://digicoll.lib.berkeley.edu.

Carey, Ryan Joseph. "Building a Better Oregon: Geographic Information and the Production of Space, 1846–1906." PhD diss., University of Texas at Austin, 2003.

Coe, Lawrence W. "Lawrence Coe to Putnam Bradford, April 6, 1856." Letter. Skamania County Historical Society. *The Cascades Massacre, Letter of L.W. Coe, Story of the Indian War at Fort Rains, W.T., 1856.* http://www.columbiagorge.org/wp-content/uploads/2013/06/Cascade_Massacre_Letter_of_l._W._Coe.pdf.

Dictation of Capt. John C. Ainsworth, 1888, P-A, 72: 1, Selections From The Bancroft Library. Bancroft Library, University of California, Berkeley. Berkeley, California. https://digicoll.lib.berkeley.edu.

Jacob Kamm Papers, 1852–1903, Mss 1451, Oregon Historical Society Research Library, Oregon Historical Society. Portland, Oregon.

Johansen, Dorothy O. "Capitalism on the Far-Western Frontier: The Oregon Steam Navigation Company." PhD diss., University of Washington, 1941.

John C. Ainsworth Papers, 1858–1911, Coll 250, Special Collections & University Archives, University of Oregon Libraries. Eugene, Oregon.

The Letters and Private Papers of Simeon Gannett Reed, 1940, F881.R4, Reed College Library. Portland, Oregon.

Skamania County. Deed, by Daniel F. Bradford, Chloe H. Bradford, Anne P. Hamlin and C.J. Palmer. Skamania County Book of Deeds, Book A, Page 13. Cascades, Washington Territory: Skamania County, 1856.

Articles

Baker, W.W. "The Building of the Walla Walla & Columbia River Railroad." *Washington Historical Quarterly* 14, no. 1 (1923): 3–13.

Gill, Frank B. "Oregon's First Railway: The Oregon Portage Railroad at the Cascades of the Columbia River." *Quarterly of the Oregon Historical Society* 25, no. 3 (1924): 171–235.

Gill, Frank B., and Dorothy O. Johansen. "A Chapter in the History of the Oregon Steam Navigation Company: The Steamship Oregonian (Part II)." *Oregon Historical Quarterly* 38, no. 3 (1937): 300–322.

———. "A Chapter in the History of the Oregon Steam Navigation Company: The Steamship Oregonian (Part IV, Continued)." *Oregon Historical Quarterly* 39, no. 1 (1938): 50–64.

———. "A Chapter in the History of the Oregon Steam Navigation Company: The Steamship Oregonian (Part III, Continued)." *Oregon Historical Quarterly* 38, no. 4 (1938): 398–410.

Gillette, P.W. "A Brief History of the Oregon Steam Navigation Company." *Quarterly of the Oregon Historical Society* 5, no. 2 (1904): 120–32.

Lyman, Lloyd Gouvy. "Simeon Gannett Reed: A Preliminary Biographical Study." Reed Digital Collections, 1948. https://rdc.reed.edu.

Oregon Spectator. "From Portland to the Dalles." February 17, 1855.

Books

Ambrose, Stephen E. *Undaunted Courage: Meriwether Lewis, Thomas Jefferson, and the Opening of the American West*. New York: Touchstone, 1996.

Chandler, Alfred D. *The Invisible Hand: The Managerial Revolution in American Business*. Cambridge, MA: Belknap Press, 1977.

De Borchgrave, Alexandra, and John Cullen. *Villard: The Life and Times of an American Titan*. New York: Nan A. Talese, 2001.

Lavender, David. *Nothing Seemed Impossible: William C. Ralston and Early San Francisco*. Palo Alto, CA: American West Publishing Company, 1975.

Levy, Jonathan. *Ages of American Capitalism: A History of the United States*. New York: Random House, 2021.

Lubetkin, M. John. *Jay Cooke's Gamble: The Northern Pacific Railroad, the Sioux, and the Panic of 1873*. Norman: University of Oklahoma Press, 2006.

MacColl, E. Kimbark. *Merchants, Money and Power*. Athens, GA: Georgian Press, 1988.

Mills, Randall V. *Stern-Wheelers Up Columbia: A Century of Steamboating in the Oregon Country*. Lincoln: University of Nebraska Press, 1947.

Newell, Gordon. *Pacific Steamboats*. Seattle, WA: Superior Publishing Company, 1958.

Oregon Railway and Navigation Company. *Annual Report of the Board of Directors of the Oregon Railway and Navigation Company, to the Stockholders, for the Year Ending June 30, 1885*. New York: Searing & Hyde, Printers, 1885.

Schafer, Joseph. *A History of the Pacific Northwest*. San Bernardino, CA: First Rate Publishers, 2014.

Schwantes, Carlos A. *Long Day's Journey: The Steamboat & Stagecoach Era in the Northern West*. Seattle: University of Washington Press, 1999.

Stevenson, Louise L. *The Victorian Homefront: American Thought and Culture, 1860–1880*. New York: Twayne Publishers, 1991.

Summers, Mark Wahlgren. *Railroads, Reconstruction, and the Gospel of Prosperity: Aid Under the Radical Republicans, 1865–1877*. Princeton, NJ: Princeton University Press, 1984.

Timmen, Fritz. *Blow for the Landing: A Hundred Years of Steam Navigation on the Waters of the West*. Atglen, PA: Schiffer Publishing, Limited, 1973.

Wright, E.W. *Marine History of the Pacific Northwest: An Illustrated Review of the Growth and Development of the Maritime Industry, from the Advent of the Earliest Navigators to the Present Time, with Sketches and Portraits of a Number of Well Known Marine Men*. Portland, OR: Lewis & Dryden Printing Company, 1895.

Newspapers

Morning Oregonian, 1861–93. www.newspapers.com.
May 13, 1861, 3; February 27, 1862, 3; May 9, 1862, 2; November 14, 1862, 2; November 22, 1862, 2; June 23, 1864, 2; August 9, 1866, 3; June 9, 1868,

2; July 8, 1869, 2; January 2, 1871, 2; January 11, 1871, 3; May 19, 1871, 3; August 12, 1871, 3; August 28, 1875, 2; January 14, 1878, 3; June 27, 1879, 2; December 31, 1893, 3.

Oakland Tribune, 1880–93. www.newspapers.com.
August 2, 1880, 1; September 16, 1880, 3; September 23, 1880, 3; June 25, 1881, 3; October 11, 1881, 3; November 1, 1881, 3; November 16, 1881, 3; March 25, 1882, 3; June 20, 1883, 3; July 28, 1883, 1; February 2, 1885, 4; September 4, 1886, 1; September 18, 1886, 10; December 4, 1886, 10; February 18, 1888, 8; May 5, 1890, 6; July 31, 1893, 8.

Oregon Daily Journal, 1907–12. www.newspapers.com.
September 15, 1907, 10; July 11, 1908, 8; January 26, 1909, 18; December 14, 1912, 1.

ABOUT THE AUTHOR

Mychal Ostler, MA, LMFT, is a native of the Columbia Gorge and grew up living and working on the river. His lifelong passion for the Oregon Steam Navigation Company and its steamboats inspired the idea for this book. His education in communication at Central Washington University has inspired his writing style, and his clinical experience as a practicing mental health counselor has informed his interpretations of the characters in the story, their personal struggles and the nature of their relationships with one another and their enemies. Mychal has written articles about the Oregon Steam Navigation Company and Columbia River steamboats for such publications as *Sea History Magazine* and *COLUMBIA Magazine*. Mychal lives with his wife, daughter and three pets in Raleigh, North Carolina. His next project is writing a biography about an Oregon pioneer.

Visit us at
www.historypress.com